FREE AUDIO EXAMPLES Available for Streaming or Download – No Signup Required!

PLAY BI

Daily Lessons 1
Rhythm and Lead Guitar in Just Two Weeks!

By Troy Nelson

HOW TO GET THE AUDIO	3		
INTRODUCTION	4		
HOW TO USE THIS BOOK	6		
WEEK 1 – DAY 1	7	WEEK 2 – DAY 8	31
DAY 2	10	DAY 9	35
DAY 3	13	DAY 10	38
DAY 4	17	DAY 11	42
DAY 5	21	DAY 12	45
DAY 6	25	DAY 13	49
DAY 7 - WEEK 1 REVIEW	29	DAY 14 - WEEK 2 REVIEW	53

ISBN 9781720038290   Copyright © 2018-2020 Troy Nelson Music
International Copyright Secured. All Rights Reserved

No part of this publication may be reproduced without the written consent of the author, Troy Nelson. Unauthorized copying, arranging, adapting, recording, Internet posting, public performance or other distribution of the printed or recorded music in this publication is an infringement of copyright. Infringers are liable under the law.

HOW TO GET THE AUDIO

The audio files for this book are available for free as downloads or streaming on *troynelsonmusic.com*.

We are available to help you with your audio downloads and any other questions you may have. Simply email *help@troynelsonmusic.com*.

See below for the recommended ways to listen to the audio:

Download Audio Files (Zipped)	Stream Audio Files
• Download Audio Files (Zipped)	• Recommended for CELL PHONES or TABLETS
• Recommended for COMPUTERS on WiFi	• Bookmark this page
• A ZIP file will automatically download to the default "downloads" folder on your computer	• Simply tap the PLAY button on the track you want to listen to
• Recommended: download to a desktop/laptop computer *first*, then transfer to a tablet or cell phone	• Files also available for streaming or download at *soundcloud.com/troynelsonbooks*
• Phones & tablets may need an "unzipping" app such as iZip, Unrar, or Winzip	
• Download on WiFi for faster download speeds	

**To download the companion audio files for this book,
visit: troynelsonmusic.com/audio-downloads/**

INTRODUCTION

Play blues guitar in 14 days?! That's impossible! If that was your initial reaction to this book, you're probably not alone. But the truth is, if you're truly dedicated to learning blues guitar, and you're willing to put in the work, you can learn all the tools you'll need to be a well-rounded and competent blues guitarist in just two weeks' time.

If you're an absolute beginner looking for a method book to teach you the fundamentals of playing guitar… well, this isn't it. Instead, *Play Blues Guitar in 14 Days* is focused on teaching you everything you need to begin playing the blues with another guitarist, singer, or even in a group setting. While the book is not written for the absolute beginner, the material does start at a level best-suited for guitarists at the "late beginner" or "early intermediate" stage. That said, *Play Blues Guitar in 14 Days* has something for everyone, including guitarists picking up the instrument for the first time or those who have played for a number of years but are unfamiliar with the blues.

The book is divided into 14 sections, one for each day of the two-week program. Within each section/day are six categories: Chords, Rhythm & Harmony, Scale, Technique, Lead Lick, and Turnaround. The goal is to spend 15 minutes playing the exercises in each category, for a total of 90 minutes (15 X 6 = 90) per day.

The day starts with an introduction to the chords that will be the focus of the rest of the day's exercises. The chords are illustrated in diagrams and then in tab, where basic rhythms are paired with the chord shapes to create exercises that will get you accustomed to the new voicings—everything from dyads and triads to dominant seventh and ninth chords.

The next 15 minutes (Rhythm & Harmony) are devoted to learning a common blues riff or rhythm figure. The voicings used here are the same ones you learned in the preceding Chords section and follow the fundamental I–IV ("one-four") blues chord progression (specifically, the first four bars of a 12-bar blues).

After a half hour of rhythm playing, the middle portion of the practice session is devoted to playing lead. The Scale section is first up and features—you guessed it—a scale. We start with everybody's favorite scale, minor pentatonic, before moving on to other scales favored by blues guitarists, including the blues scale, major pentatonic, and even more advanced scales like the Mixolydian and Dorian modes. All 15 minutes of this section are dedicated to getting comfortable with the scale pattern, playing it several times in ascending and descending fashion in preparation for the forthcoming sections, where the scale will be implemented. In fact, the next section, Technique, puts the scale to work immediately. Here, we'll cover some of the most important technical aspect of the genre—string bending, slides, hammer-ons and pull-offs, vibrato, etc.—while using the notes from that day's scale.

The 90-minute practice session wraps up with the final two sections: Lead Lick and Turnaround. The former introduces a lead phrase that can be used to solo over the rhythm figure that was presented in the Rhythm & Harmony section, using the scale and technique that you learned in the previous two sections. For example, on Day 1, E minor pentatonic (Scale) and hammer-ons (Technique) are used to create a four-bar lead phrase to be played over the I–IV (E–A) progression that was introduced in the Rhythm & Harmony section. This is where everything you've been learning in the practice session—the chords, the scale, the technique—comes together.

But we're not quite done yet. The final 15 minutes of the practice section is devoted to a staple of blues music, the turnaround. The turnaround occurs in the final two bars of the standard 12-bar blues song form and involves movement from the I chord to the V chord and building tension that is ultimately released when the progression moves back to the I chord in bar 1 (hence the term "turnaround"). The chord changes can vary a bit, but the V chord usually appears last. Over the past century, blues guitarists have created countless ways to handle these changes, some of which have become standard practice. We'll focus on a dozen of these turnarounds in this section of the book.

After six straight days of 90-minute practice sessions, the seventh (and 14th) day is dedicated to reviewing the material that was presented throughout the week. Here, you'll get your first opportunity to test-drive the scales, rhythms, chords, and techniques, as one of the week's rhythm figures is extrapolated over the entire 12-bar blues form, with a sample solo included to demonstrate how the techniques and scales can be combined to create lead phrases that handle each of the chord changes with authority and authenticity.

HOW TO USE THIS BOOK

Granted, 90 minutes of practice per day can seem daunting to some, especially if you are unaccustomed to practices sessions lasting longer than 20–30 minutes. And that's OK! Just because the book is structured to teach you blues guitar in 14 days doesn't mean you have to follow the program precisely. On the contrary, if you have, say, 30 minutes to devote to the book each day, then simply extend each section to a three-day practice session. The material is there for you to use, whether you get through the book in 14 days or 40.

While the 14-day plan is the goal, it's probably unrealistic for some. The important thing is to stick with it, because the material in this book will have you playing the blues with confidence and credibility. How quickly just depends on the amount of time you're able to spend on getting there.

Before you begin your daily sessions, however, I suggest spending at least 15–20 minutes listening to the accompanying audio to get a feel for the forthcoming exercises, as well as reading through each section's introduction to better understand the material you're about to learn. That way, you can spend the full 90 minutes (or however much time you have to practice that day) practicing the actual exercises.

To help you keep track of time in your practice sessions, time codes are included throughout the book. Simply set the timer on your smart phone to 90 minutes (1:30)—or however much time you can dedicate to your session—and move on to a new category every 15 minutes. Or, you can set the timer to 15 minutes (0:15) and move on to the next category when the timer goes off.

Next, set your metronome (or click track or drum loop) to a tempo at which you can play the exercise all the way through without making too many mistakes (40–50 beats per minute is probably a good starting point for most exercises). Once you're able to play the exercise cleanly, increase your tempo by 4–5 BPM. Again, make sure you can play through the exercise without making too many mistakes. If the speed is too fast, back off a bit until your execution is precise. Continue to increase your tempo incrementally until it's time to move on to the next section.

There will be times when the timer goes off but you feel like you didn't adequately learn the material. When this happens, I suggest moving on to the next category nonetheless. It may seem counterintuitive, but it's better to continue to progress through the book than to prolonging the practice time while trying to perfect the material. After you've completed the book, you can always go back and review the exercises. In fact, I recommend it. Making steady progress, while not always perfectly, keeps you mentally sharp and motived. Focusing too much on any one exercise is a sure way to sidetrack your sessions.

Lastly—and this is important—if you ever feel yourself getting physically fatigued or pain develops in any part of your body, especially your hands or arms, immediately take a break until the discomfort subsides, whether it's for 10 minutes, an hour, or for the rest of the day. You never want to push yourself beyond your physical limits and cause permanent damage. As mentioned earlier, the material isn't going anywhere; you can always go back to it when you're feeling 100%.

WEEK 1
DAY 1

CHORDS (1:30–1:15)

Countless blues riffs and rhythm patterns are based on the simple two-note chords shown below. Use the index and ring fingers of your fret hand for the fretted pitches, starting on string 5 (E5 and E6) and then shifting to string 4 (A5 and A6). The first exercise is played in a half-note rhythm, whereby each chord gets two beats. In exercise 2, the rhythm shifts to a quarter-note pulse, so be sure to cut the rhythmic durations in half (i.e., to one beat apiece).

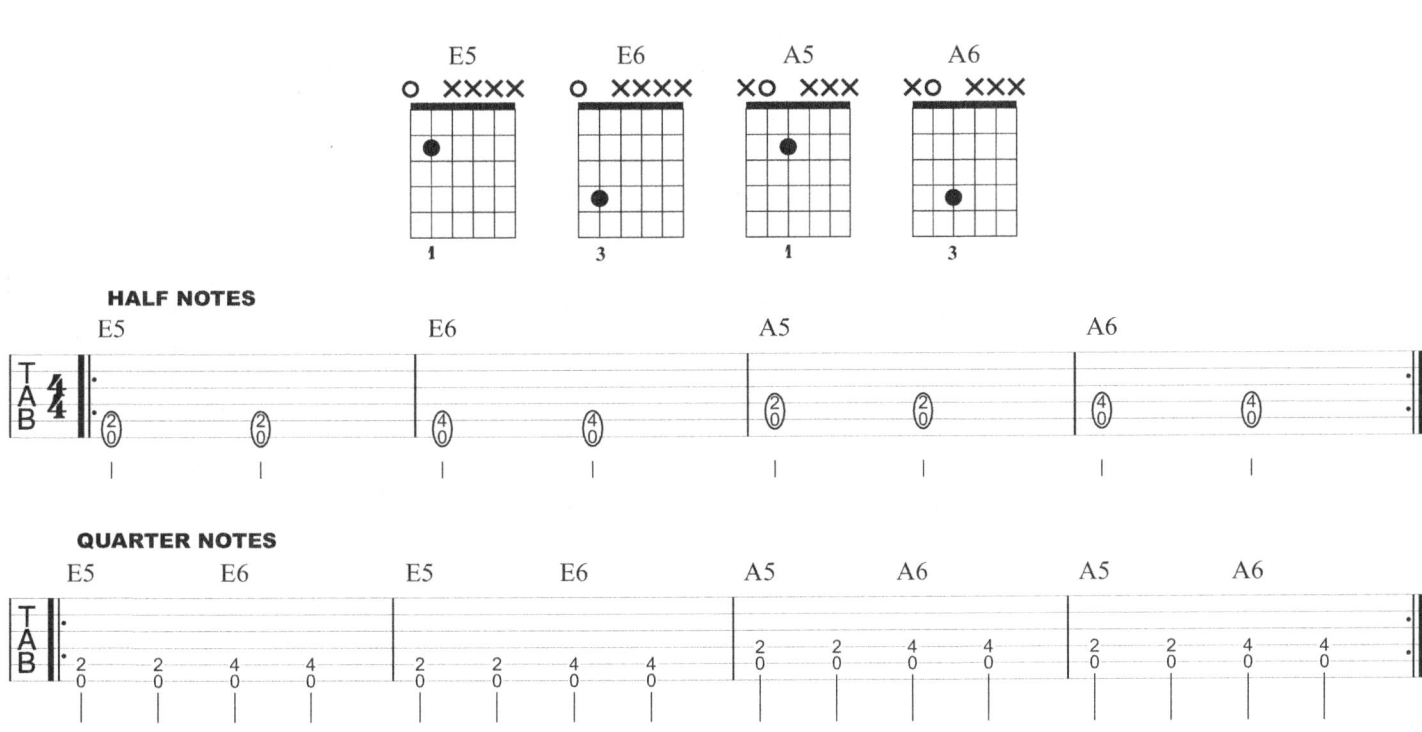

RHYTHM & HARMONY (1:15–1:00)

This rhythm figure is a blues shuffle and one of the most common blues accompaniments you will ever encounter. The figure is played in continuous eighth notes, which means the chords are strummed on both the downbeat and the upbeat of each beat. Also note the shuffle rhythm indicator in parentheses above the tab staff. This indicates that the eight notes are to be shuffled rather than played as straight eighths. To do this, simply play the first eighth note of each eighth-note pair slightly longer than the second. (Listen to the audio to hear the swung eight notes in action.)

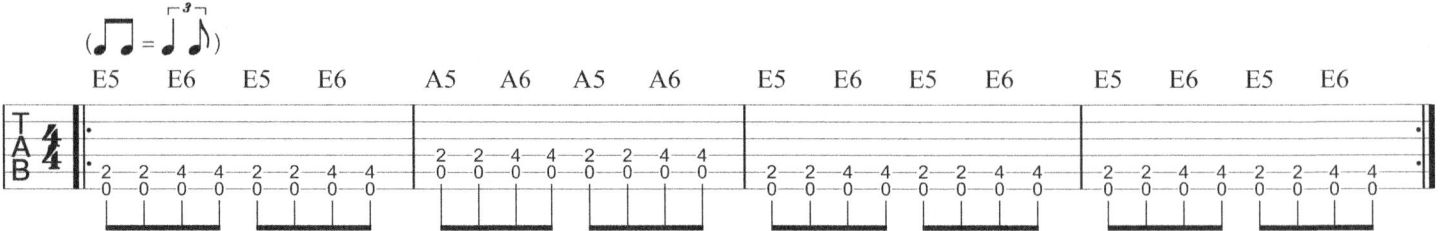

SCALE (1:00–0:45)

This scale, E minor pentatonic in open position, is perhaps the most frequently used scale in the blues. Set your metronome to a slow tempo—say, 40 BPM—and practice ascending and descending the scale several times, increasing your speed when your able to play through the scale flawlessly at your current tempo. Repeat. Pay special attention to the root notes (circled), as they are the most important note of the scale and act as "guideposts" when learning scales.

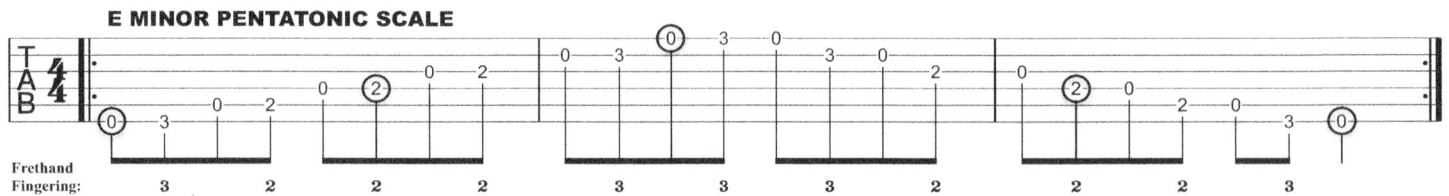

TECHNIQUE (0:45–0:30)

This exercise combines the scale we just learned, E minor pentatonic, and our first technique, hammer-ons. To play the hammer-ons, simply pluck the first note on each string and "hammer" your fret-hand finger onto the second note (without re-striking the string with your pick). Be careful not to rush the hammer-ons, which is easy to do. The pick attacks should fall directly on the downbeats, with the hammer-ons occurring precisely on the upbeats. Listen to the audio to hear them in action.

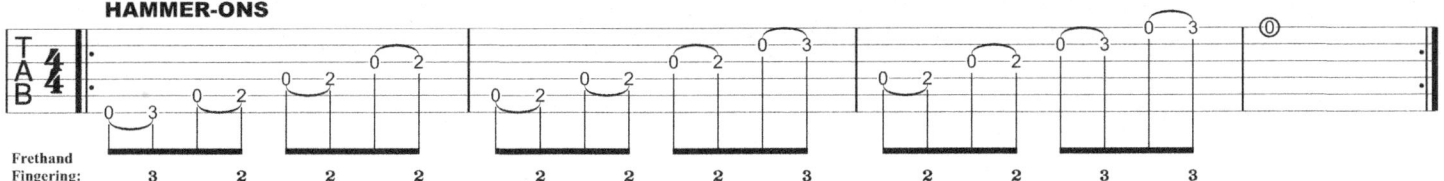

LEAD LICK (0:30–0:15)

Our first lick involves playing over the chord progression from earlier in the section, E–A–E (I–IV–I). The phrase gets its notes from our open-position E minor pentatonic scale and uses hammer-ons liberally throughout. Two things to be aware of: 1) there's a pickup measure, which begins on the upbeat of beat 3, and 2) the eighth notes are swung.

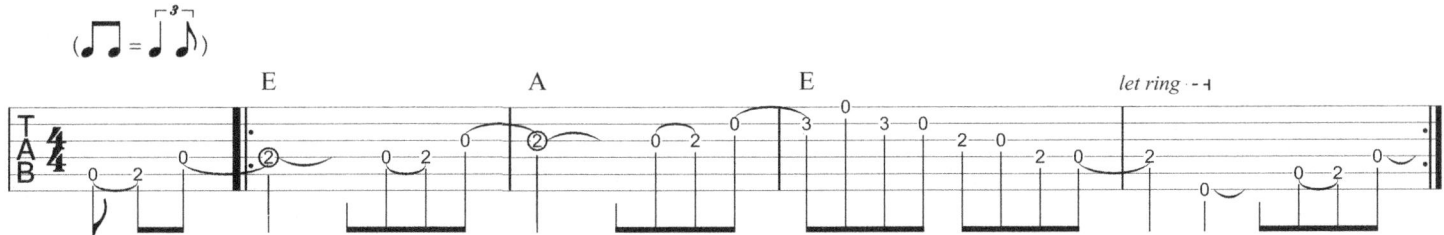

TURNAROUND (0:15–0:00)

This is a popular phrase amongst blues guitarists for navigating a turnaround in the key of E. After plucking the open low-E string on beat 1, chromatically descending notes on string 2 are played against the open high-E string. This is followed by a walk up string 5 to the B note at fret 2, which is the root of the V ("five") chord.

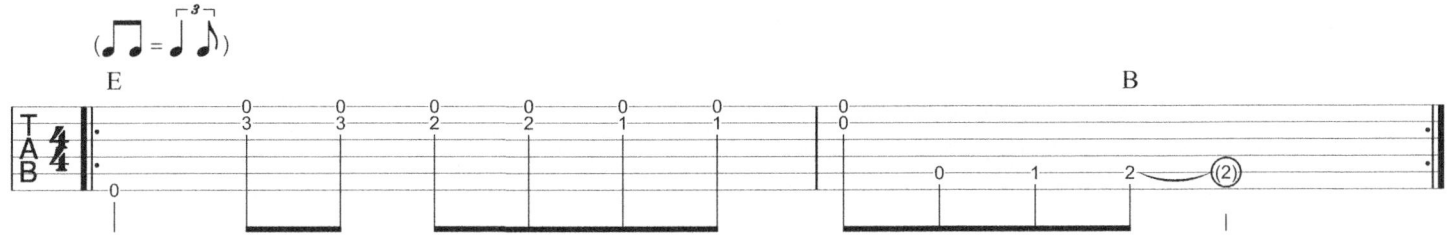

DAY 2

CHORDS (1:30–1:15)

Two new chords, E7 and A7, are introduced here (the others are carryovers from Day 1). These new voicings allow us to extend our E5–E6 (and A5–A6) shuffle pattern to include the 7th chord, which is highly desirable in the blues. If the pinky proves too difficult for the E7 and A7 chords, you can substitute your ring finger, sliding it from fret 4 to fret 5 and back. Again, we start with half notes in the first exercise before moving on to quarter notes in exercise 2.

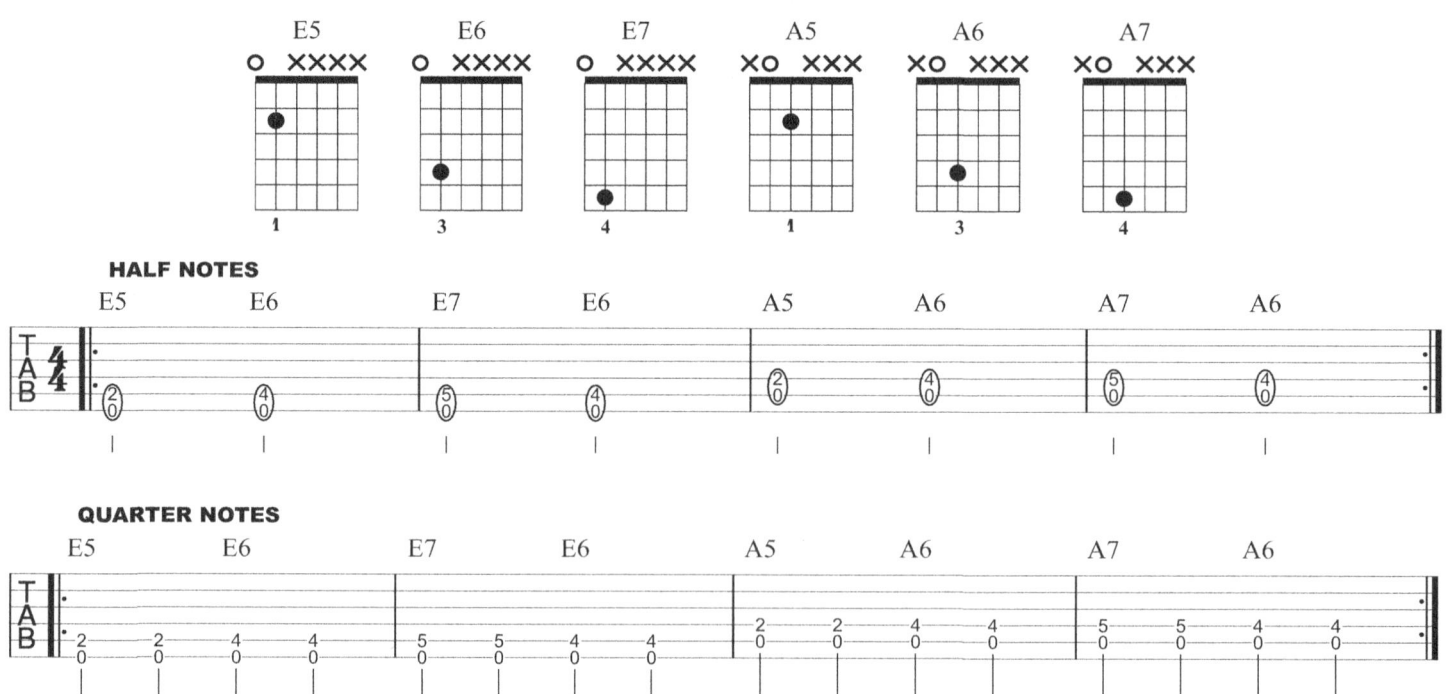

RHYTHM & HARMONY (1:15–1:00)

Here's the shuffle pattern with the 7th chord, played over the I–IV–I progression. Remember to shuffle the eighth notes! And, as before, if your pinky struggles to keep up, just use your ring finger and slide back and forth between frets 4 and 5.

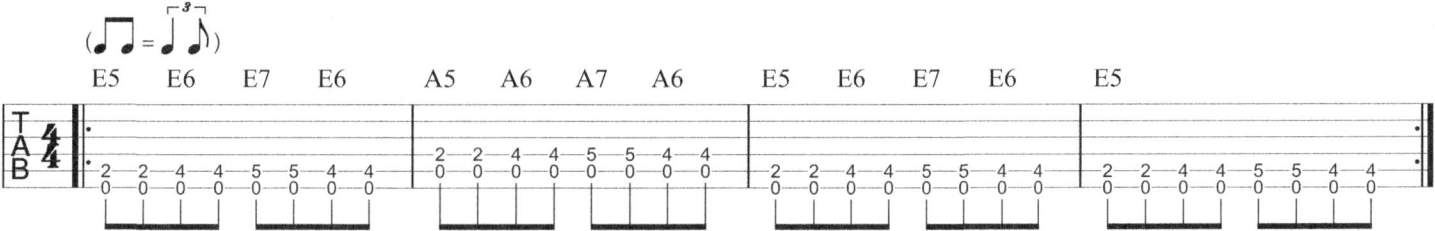

SCALE (1:00–0:45)

This scale is the fretted version of our open-position E minor pentatonic. Guitarists love this scale because of the symmetry of the pattern—specifically, the index/pinky and index/ring combinations that are employed throughout. This shape is one of several pentatonic "box" patterns found along the fretboard, but it's the one that gets the most mileage!

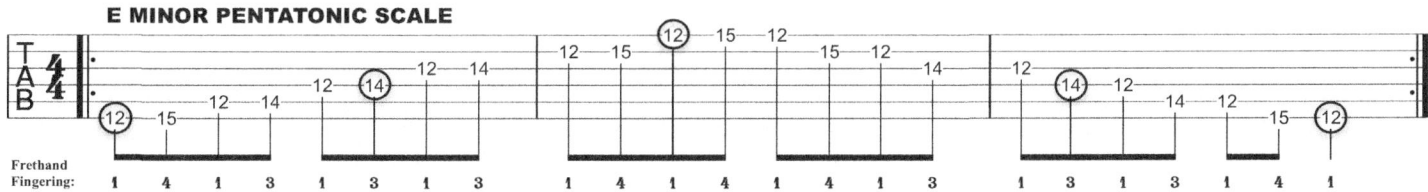

TECHNIQUE (0:45–0:30)

Pull-offs are similar to hammer-ons but in reverse order; that is, instead off sounding the second note of each two-note pair by hammering onto the string, a pull-off involves plucking the string with your pick and then pulling off from the string with a slight downward motion of your frethand finger—sort of like a frethand pluck. In the exercise below, the 12th-position E minor pentatonic scale is descended entirely with pull-offs, in a repetitive four-note pattern.

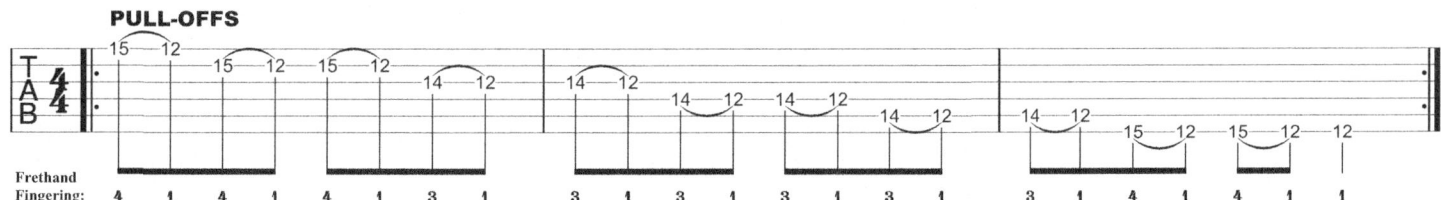

LEAD LICK (0:30–0:15)

This four-bar phrase, played over our familiar I–IV–I (E–A–E) progression, incorporates the 12th-position E minor pentatonic scale, several pull-offs, and a well-placed hammer-on in measure 3. Notice how the line emphasizes certain notes as the chords change, most notably the A note (root of the IV chord) at fret 14 of string 3 in bar 2 and the E note (root of the I chord) at fret 14 of string 4 in bar 3.

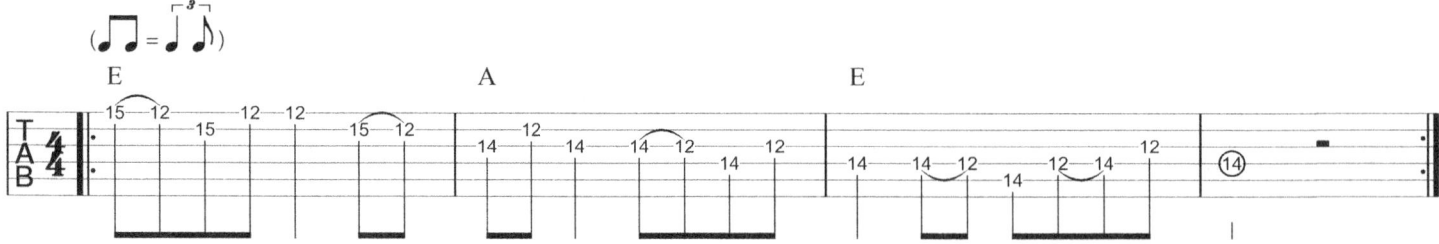

TURNAROUND (0:15–0:00)

This turnaround is a variation of the one from yesterday. Instead of plucking string 1–2 as "dyads," the top two strings are arpeggiated and allowed to ring together. Bar 2, however, is exactly the same as the version from yesterday, including the fifth-string walkup to the root of the B chord.

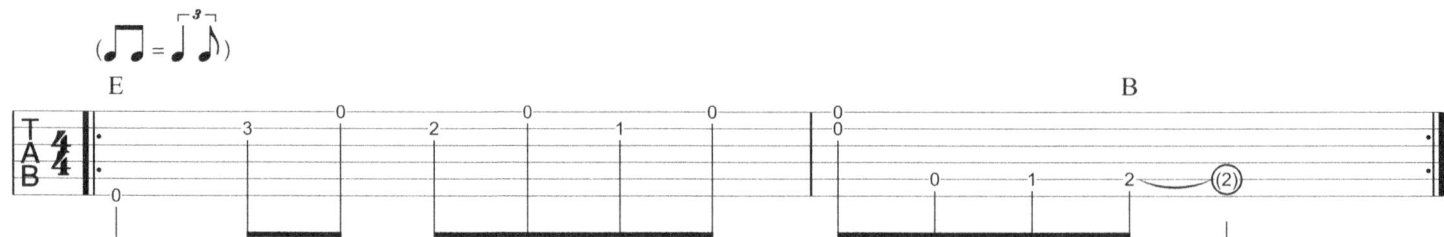

DAY 3

CHORDS (1:30–1:15)

Now that you're familiar with the two-note chords used in blues shuffles, it's time to learn some important fully fretted open-position triads and 7th chords—E, E7, A, and A7. We'll start by strumming them in half notes before moving on to quarter and eighth notes. Remember to use a metronome, playing each rhythm several times (cleanly!) before moving on to the next. These exercises will help prepare us for the blues riff that's coming up next.

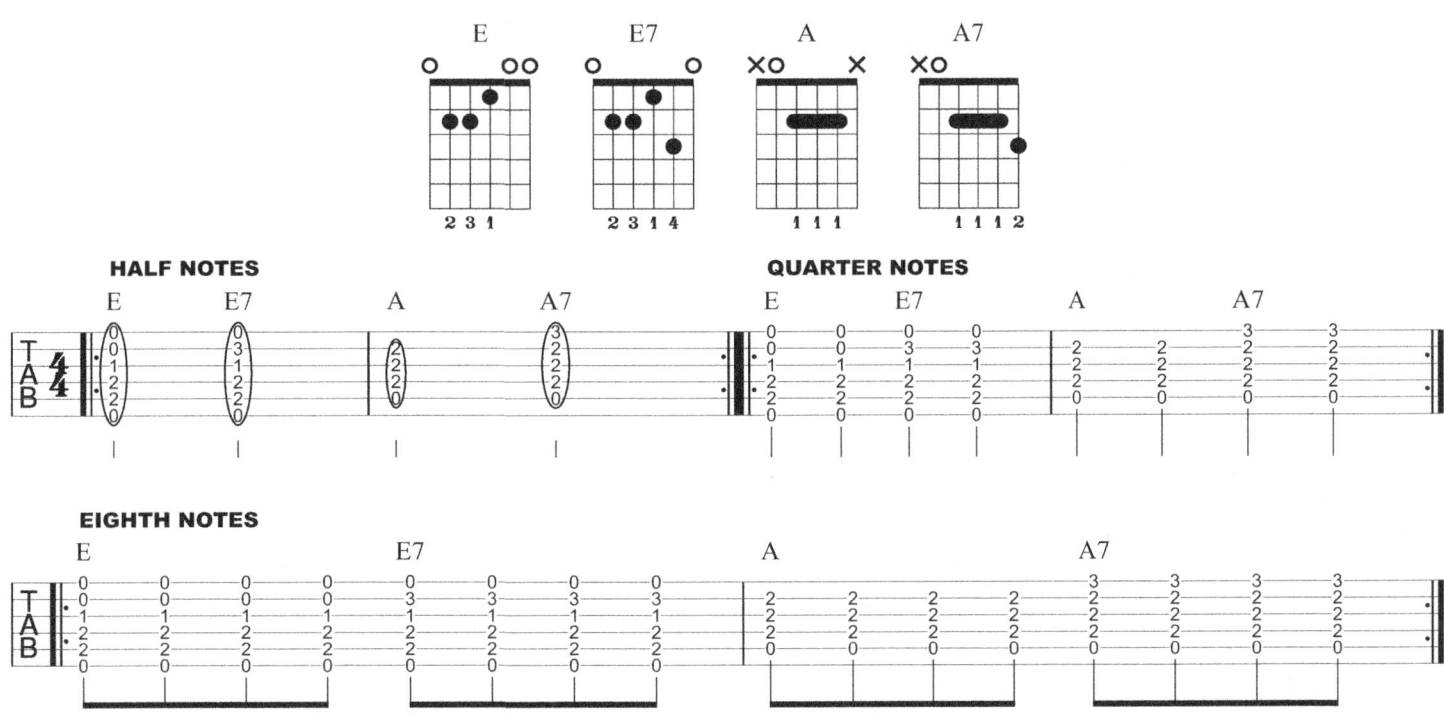

RHYTHM & HARMONY (1:15–1:00)

This blues riff is equal parts Muddy Waters and Stevie Ray Vaughan. After a pickup bass-string run, the riff goes into the major and dominant 7th voicings we learned in the Chords section. After four bars of the I (E) chord, the progression shifts to the IV (A) chord for two measures—exactly the type of changes you might experience in the first six bars of a 12-bar blues. Notice how moving from the major triad to the 7th chord gives the riff more blues cred than if we simply stayed on the major chord.

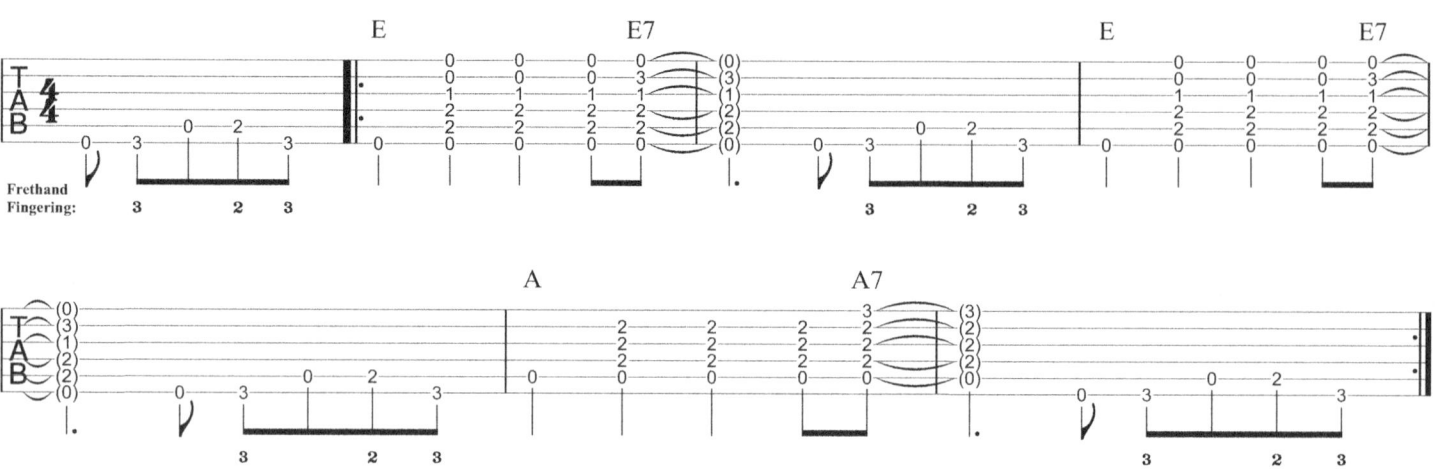

SCALE (1:00–0:45)

Back in Day 1, we learned the open-position E minor pentatonic scale. Here, we're going to learn a variation of that scale, E blues, which is used about as frequently as its predecessor. What differentiates the two scales is a single note, Bb, also known as the b5th ("flat fifth"). But this one note makes a huge difference in the sonic quality of the scale because of the intervallic relationship between it and the root of the scale. This root–b5th, or "tritone," relationship is one of the defining sounds of the blues. In the open-position pattern below, Bb is found in two locations: at fret 1 of string 5 and at fret 3 of string 3.

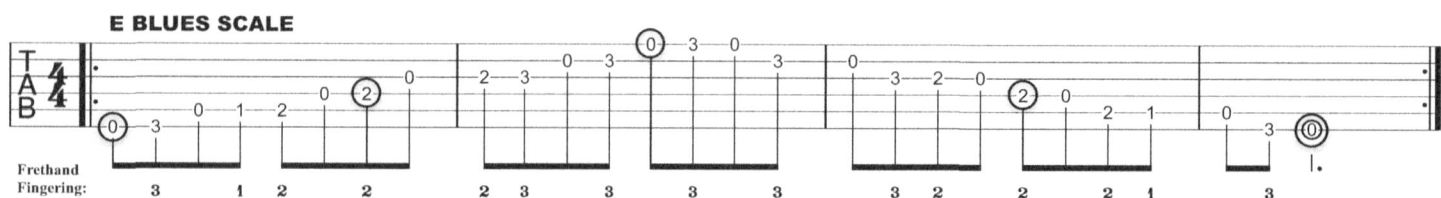

TECHNIQUE (0:45–0:30)

Today's technique is slides, or, more specifically, legato slides. A *legato slide* involves shifting a fret-hand finger up or down the fretboard from one fret to another without re-striking the string (*shift slides* involve picking both the original note and the "destination" note). Legato slides are often combined with hammer-ons and pull-offs to impart a fluid quality to licks and, in some cases, to make performance easier. Below are a couple of exercises that incorporate all three techniques. The first exercise ascends and descends the first half of our open-position E blues scale, while the second one does the same with the second half of the scale. Be sure to pay strict attention to your timing. In other words, don't rush!

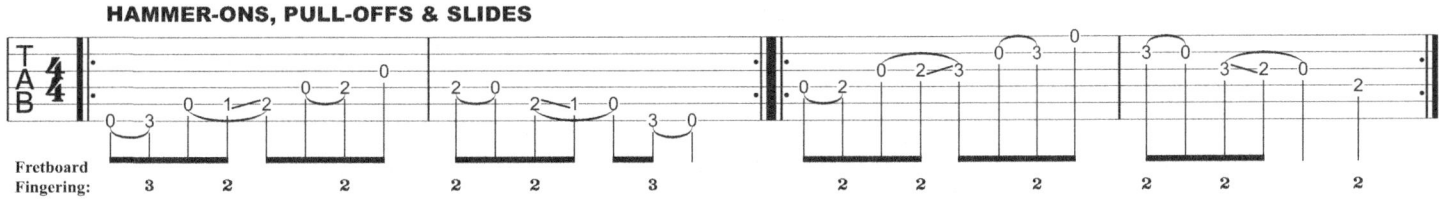

LEAD LICK (0:30–0:15)

This six-bar phrase is played over the blues riff we learned in the Rhythm & Harmony section. The line gets its pitches from the open-position E blues scale that we just learned and incorporates all of the techniques we've learned so far—hammer-ons, pull-offs, and slides. It's fairly easy to perform, but it's a bit on the long side, so don't feel like you need to memorize it in one sitting. Instead, concentrate on playing it in time and without making too many mistakes. The main goal right now is to get comfortable with playing—not memorizing—these types of lead lines and hearing how the color of the line morphs as the chords change underneath.

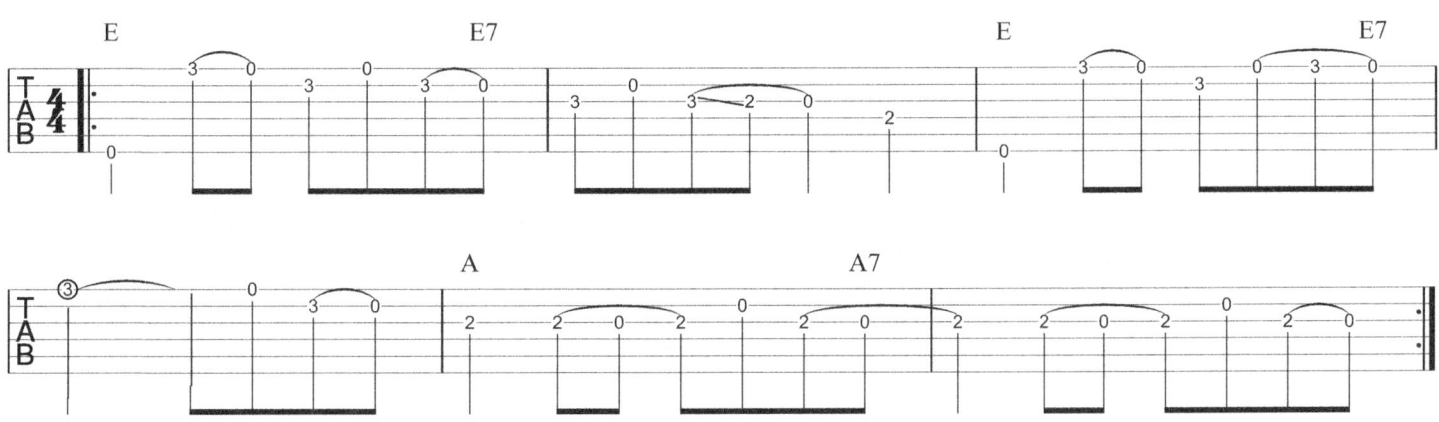

TURNAROUND (0:15–0:00)

This turnaround is a bit different from the ones we learned on Days 1 and 2 in that no single notes are involved—it's all chords. The progression here is I–IV–I–V (E–A–E–B), a very common set of chord changes for a blues turnaround. There's one new chord here, B7, which is tricky for just about every guitarist at first. If it is too difficult initially, you can pair it down to just the bottom three notes, which are voiced with the middle, index, and ring fingers, low to high. Once you have this streamlined version under your fingers, you can try adding your pinky to the F# note at fret 2 of string 1 and strum all five strings.

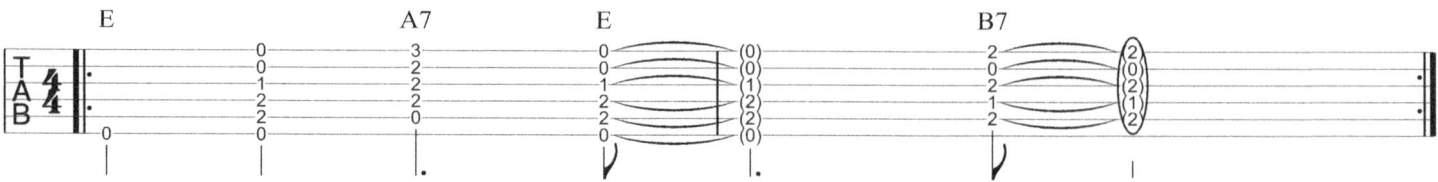

DAY 4

CHORDS (1:30–1:15)

This set of chords (E, E6, E7, A7, and A13) is sort of the open-chord version of the blues shuffles you learned back on Days 1 and 2. Here, however, the movement within the chords is occurring on strings 2 and 1 rather than on strings 5 and 4 (and the chords are more robust, of course). The E chords are based on the open-position E major voicing, while the A chords are based on a common open-position A7 voicing (don't let the A13 chord scare you; it's just a 7th chord with an extra note on top, F#). Both sets of chords are practiced in isolation, starting with half notes and ending with quarter notes. Give each of the four exercises equal time and attention, as they will prepare you well for the rhythm figure in the forthcoming section.

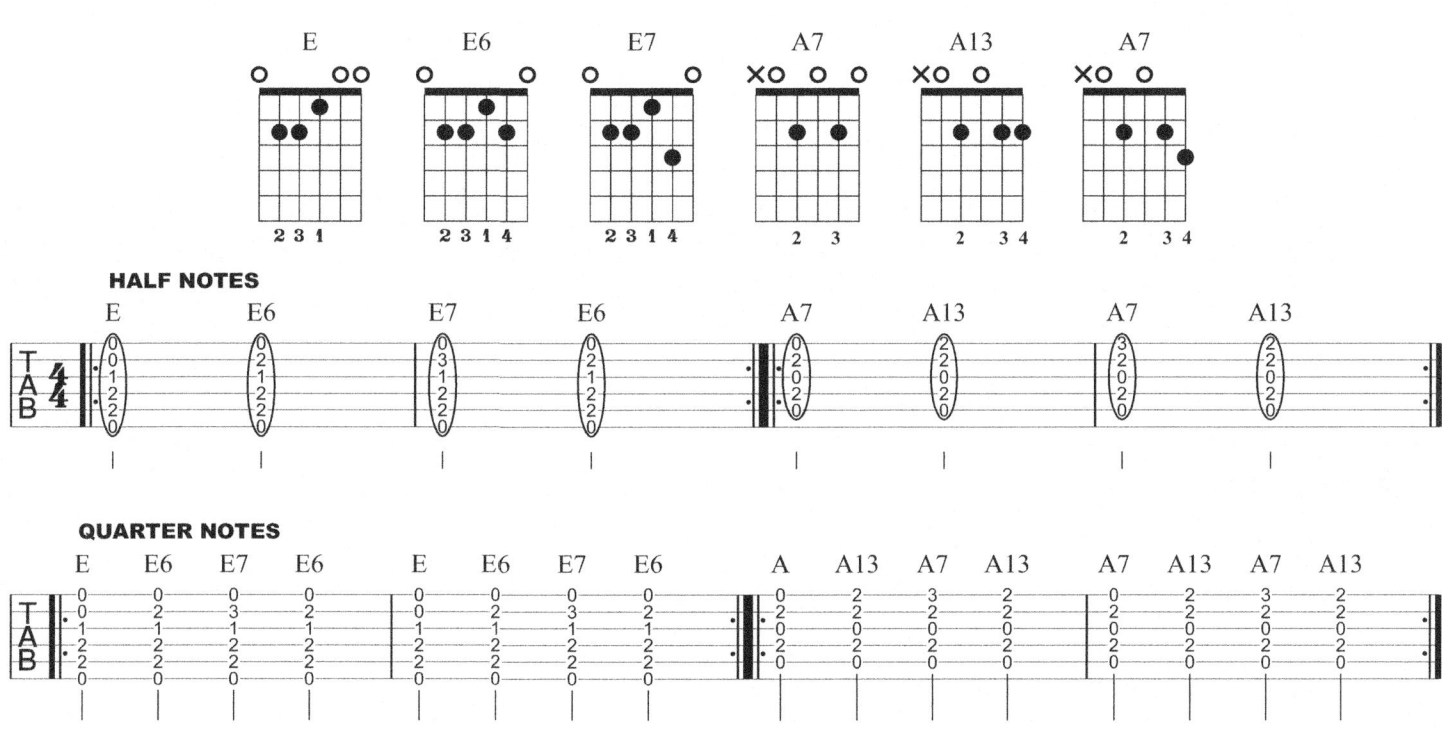

RHYTHM & HARMONY (1:15–1:00)

The voicings that we learned in the Chords section are now applied to the first four bars of a 12-bar blues, with the IV (A) chord change occurring in bar 2, and the I (E) chord occupying measures 1, 3, and 4. Rhythmically, the chords are strummed in an eighth-note shuffle pattern throughout. For best results, try alternate strumming (down-up, down-up, etc.) the entire example. Although you can use downstrums exclusively, too, the shuffle rhythm is a little more difficult to achieve this way.

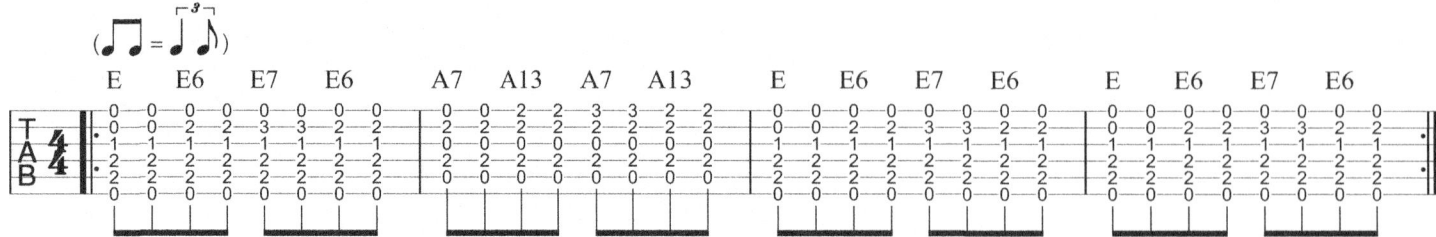

SCALE (1:00–0:45)

Yesterday, we learned the open-position E blues scale. Now, we're going to focus on the fully fretted version at fret 12. The pattern is exactly the same, but now the notes are an octave higher. Also, since you know the 12th-position E minor pentatonic scale, all you have to do is add the b5th (Bb) to strings 5 and 3.

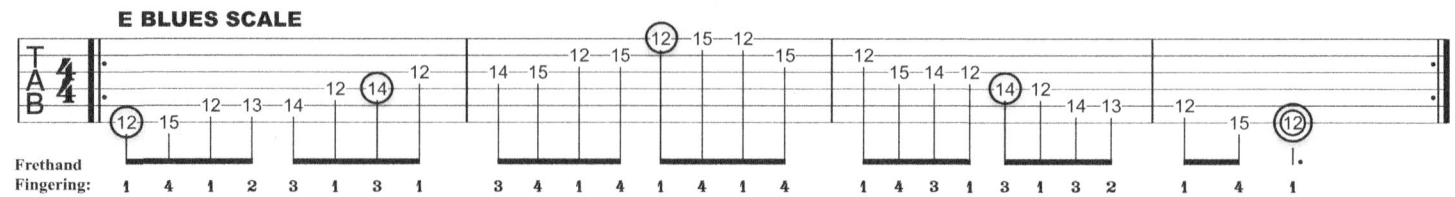

TECHNIQUE (0:45–0:30)

Today's technique is the whole-step bend and the whole-step bend and release. The first exercise below involves bending a whole step the D note at fret 15 of string 2. Use either your ring finger or your pinky to perform the bend, reinforcing the former with your middle finger and the latter with your middle and ring fingers. To ensure that we're hitting the target note, E, we're going to fret that pitch on string 1 (fret 12) and allow them to ring together. Repeat this process for exercise 2. This time, however, the best choice for the bend is your ring finger (reinforced with the middle finger, as well).

Once you've played through the first two examples several times, at several different tempos, move on to exercises 3 and 4, which involve releasing the bent notes to their original pitches. This time, we don't have the luxury of a "target pitch" on the adjacent string, so we'll have to let our ears guide us. Also, these bends can be tricky to play in time, so listen to the accompanying audio to hear them preformed properly.

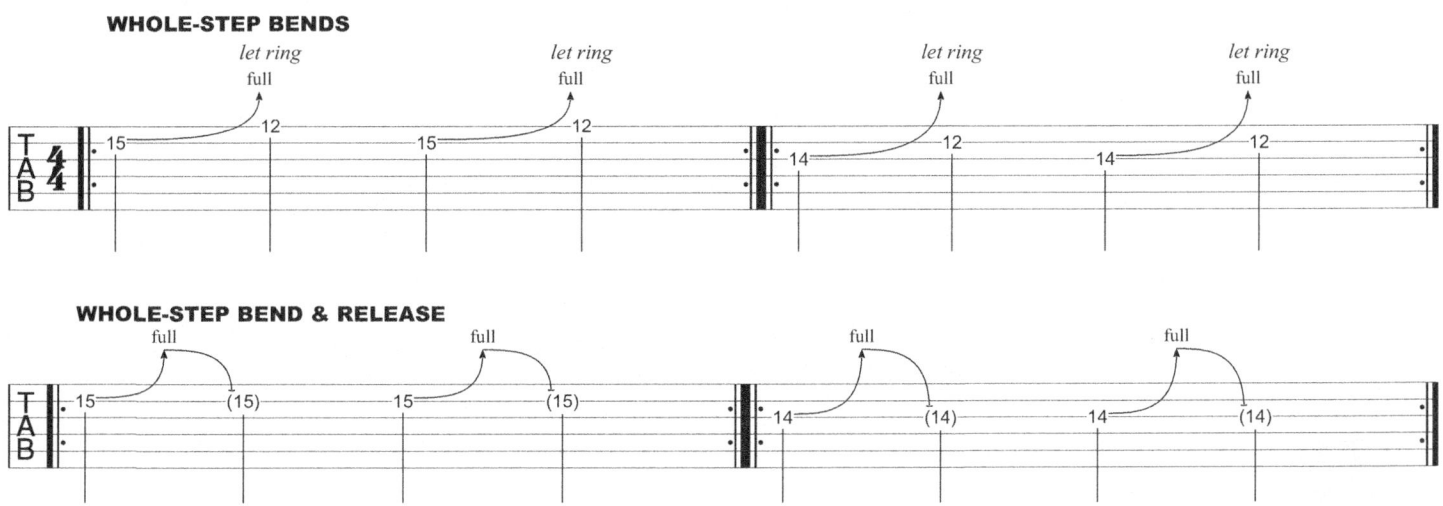

LEAD LICK (0:30–0:15)

This four-bar lead lick, played over our trusty I–IV–I (E–A–E) progression, is rooted in the 12th-position E blues scale and incorporates all of the techniques we've learned so far—hammer-ons, pull-offs, slides, and whole-step bends. Remember to swing the eighth notes (check the audio to hear them in action) and listen to how the chord changes color the line.

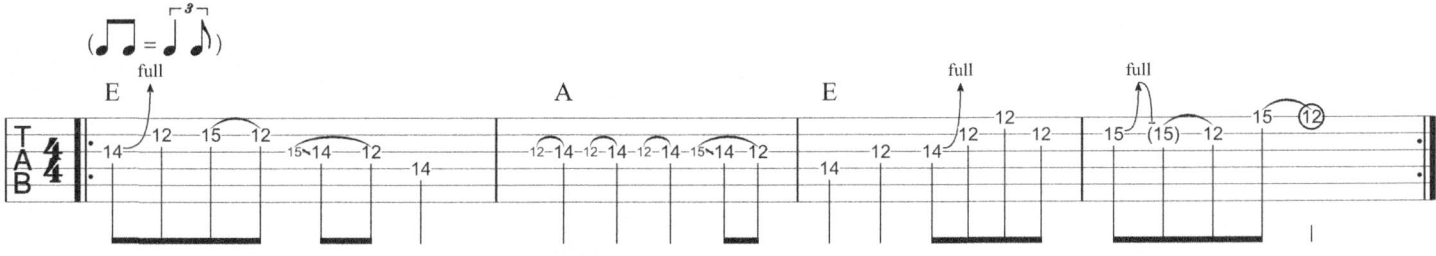

TURNAROUND (0:15–0:00)

This turnaround is similar to the one we learned on Day 2, only the descending line here occurs on string 3 rather than string 2. Another difference is the grace-note hammer-on from G to G# on beat 1 of measure 2. At first glance, it may seem like a minor detail, but this maneuver (hammering from the minor 3rd to the major 3rd) is the essence of the blues, so don't overlook it. The rest of the turnaround should look quite familiar, as it's the same walkup to the V (B) chord that we used on Days 1 and 2.

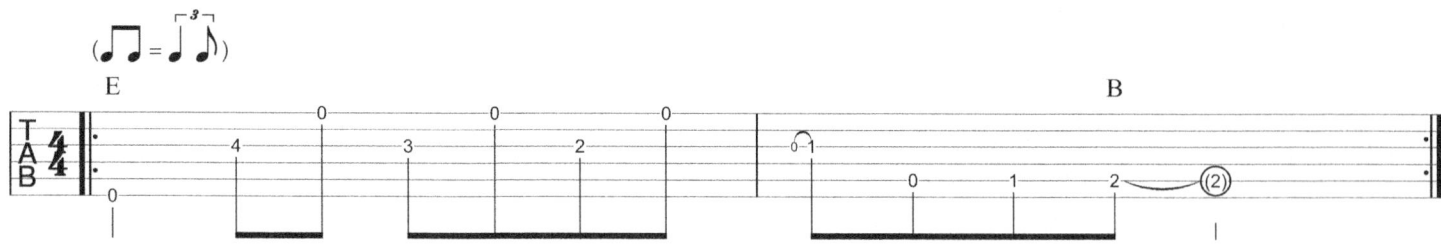

DAY 5

CHORDS (1:30–1:15)

The chords below are triads voiced exclusively on strings 2–4. The A and D voicings are pretty straightforward, while the D/A and G/D chords are voiced with a ring-finger barre. It may seem odd at first, but when we get to the blues riff in the next section, it'll become clear. When moving from A to D/A or from D to G/D, we're playing mini I–IV progressions in the keys of A major (A–D) and D major (D–G), respectively. By using a ring-finger barre, we can make the changes quicker and more efficiently. The first two exercises utilize half notes, while the last two examples feature quarter notes. Play through each of them several times, increasing the tempo incrementally.

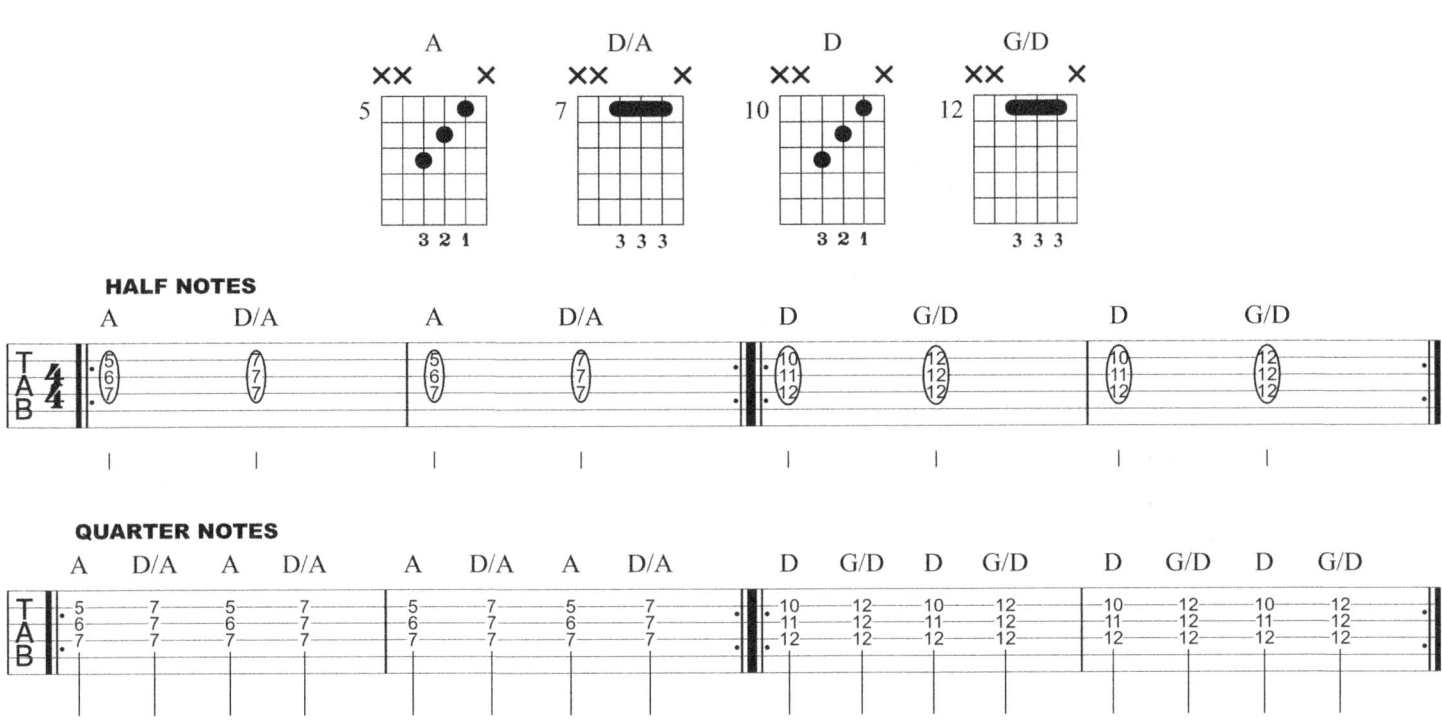

RHYTHM & HARMONY (1:15–1:00)

This bluesy riff is based on the chord voicings that we just learned, but instead of playing them as full triads, we're going to break them up into double stops (strings 2–3) and single notes (string 4), with the former falling on the downbeats and the latter falling on the upbeats. Although the mini I–IV progressions are occurring in each measure, the main I–IV–I progression (A–D–A) is still intact: measure 1 = I chord, measure 2 = IV chord, and measures 3–4 = I chord. The best way to perform this riff is to use hybrid picking, plucking the notes on string 4 with your pick, and the notes on strings 3–2 with your middle and ring fingers, respectively.

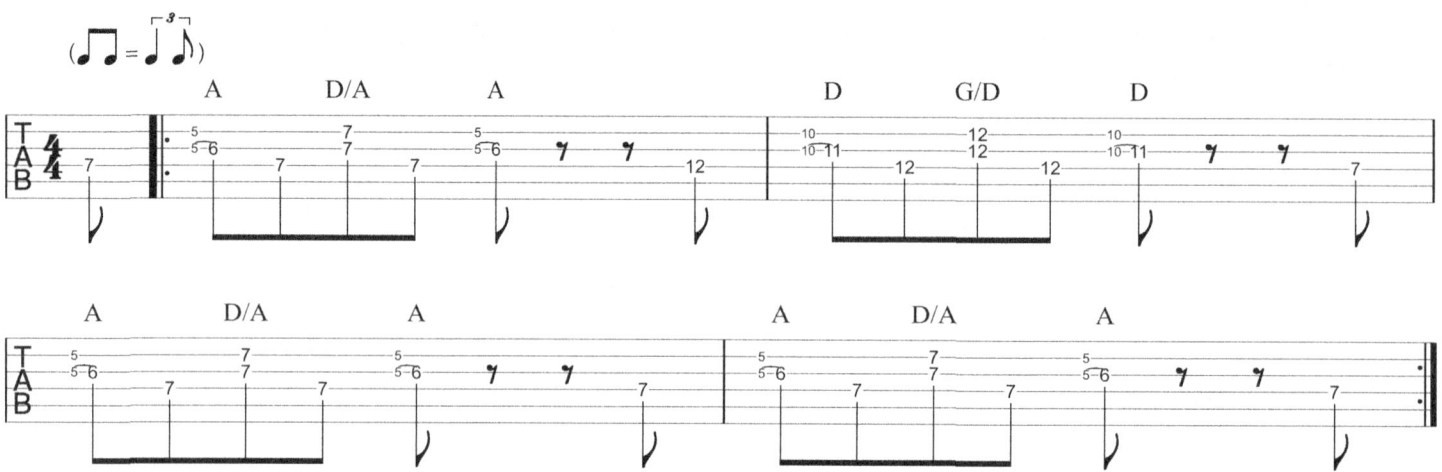

SCALE (1:00–0:45)

Up to this point, the scales that we've learned (E minor pentatonic and E blues) have been minor in quality. In this section, we're going to learn our first major scale—A major pentatonic. The great thing about minor and major pentatonic scales is that, once you've learned the finger pattern for one of them, learning a second pattern is unnecessary because they share the same notes—they're the same scale! In music theory, any two scales that share the same notes are relative scales, and every minor scale has a relative major, and vice versa. In this case, A major pentatonic is the relative major of F# minor pentatonic (G major pentatonic is the relative major of our E minor pentatonic scales from earlier).

The pattern below is exactly the same as the E minor pentatonic scale that we learned on Day 2, only we're playing it in a different position (because they're not relative) and the tonics (roots) are found in different locations—specifically, at fret 5 of strings 6 and 1 and on fret 2 of string 3.

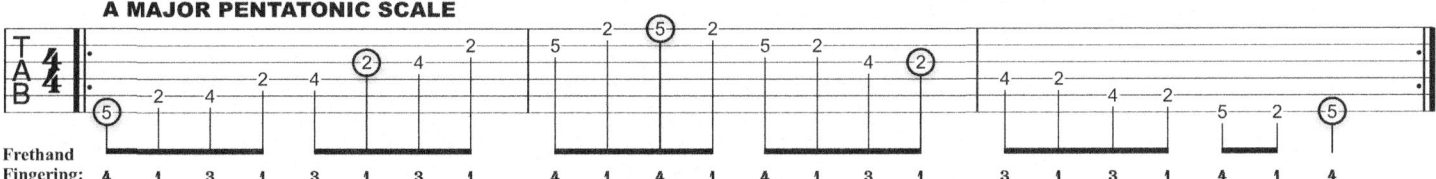

TECHNIQUE (0:45–0:30)

Yesterday, we focused on the whole-step bend and release. Today, we're shifting our attention to the whole-step *pre*-bend and release. A pre-bend is a string that is bent to its destination—in this case, a whole step—before the string is plucked. Then, the string can be held at this bent pitch or it can be released to its original, pre-bent pitch. The exercises below feature some common whole-step bends, pre-bends, and releases within the context of the A major pentatonic scale that we just learned.

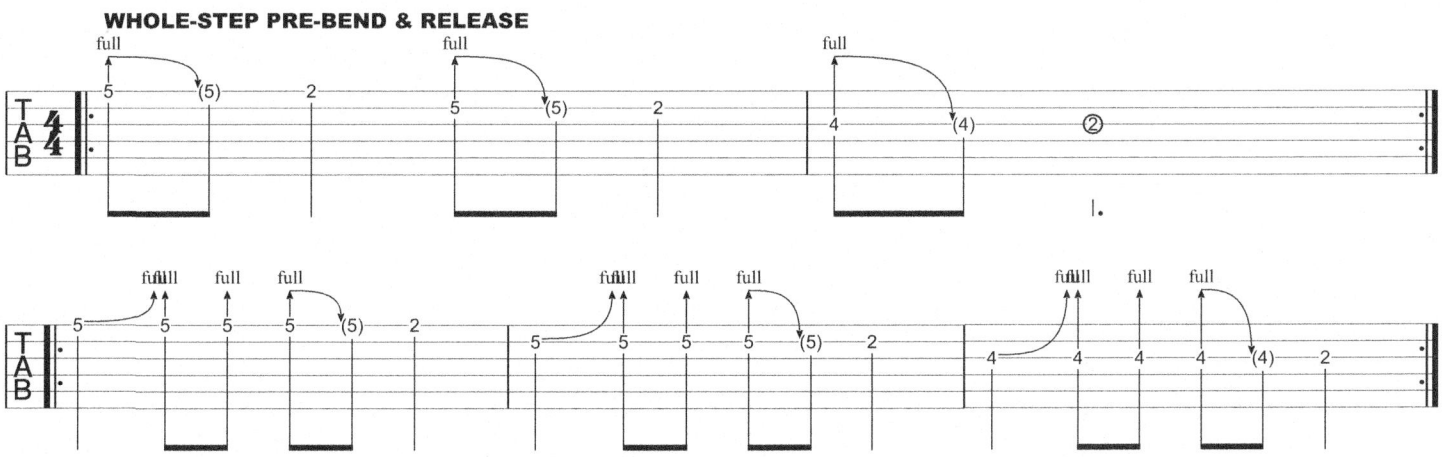

LEAD LICK (0:30–0:15)

Here's a four-bar phrase that can be played over the double-stop riff that we learned in the Rhythm & Harmony section. The entire lick is rooted in the A major pentatonic scale pattern that we just learned and features several techniques that we've encountered over the past few days, including whole-step bends and pre-bends, hammer-ons, and pull-offs.

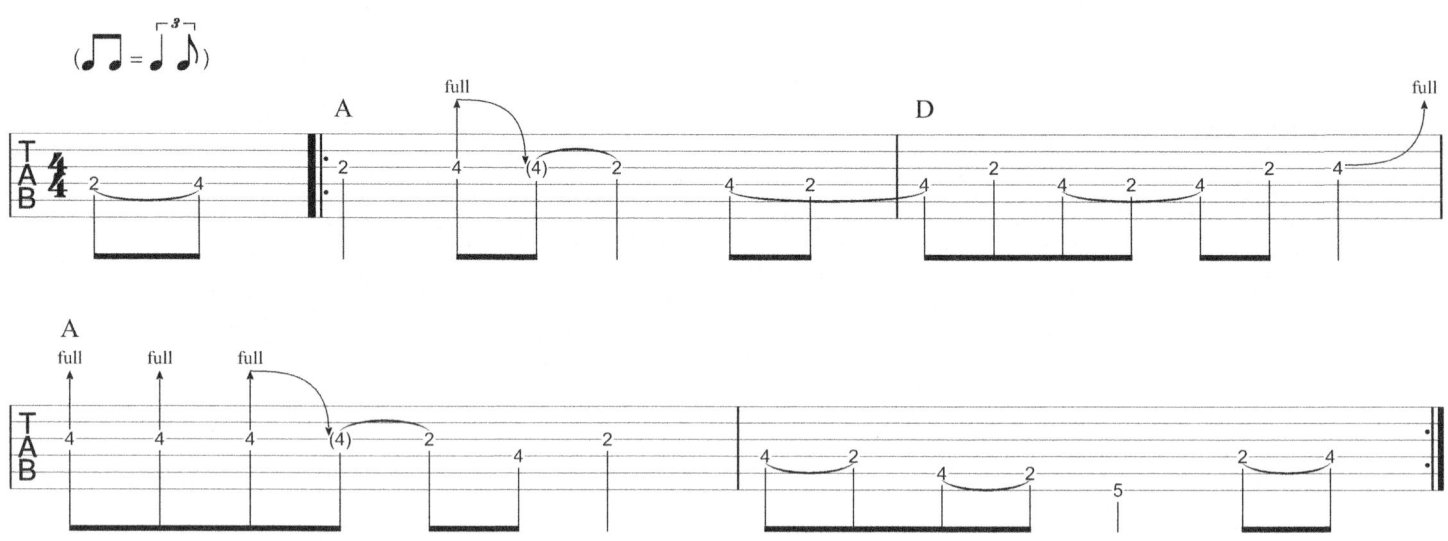

TURNAROUND (0:15–0:00)

This turnaround differs from the previous turnarounds that we've learned in that it's in the key of A (rather than the key of E), so the second half of it walks up to E, the root of our new V chord, instead of B. Meanwhile, the first part of the turnaround has a similar string 3-to-string 1 descending pattern as the turnaround in Day 4; however, this phrase features chromatically descending major 6th intervals in place of the open high-E string.

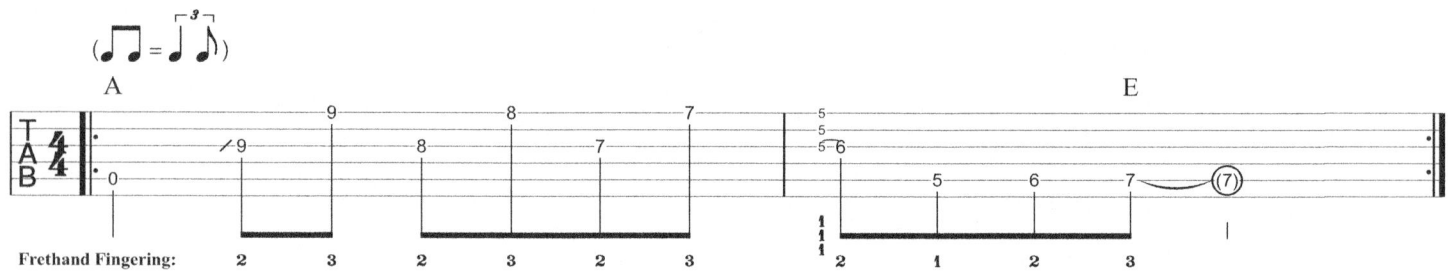

DAY 6

CHORDS (1:30–1:15)

Two of the three chords shapes in these exercises should already be familiar, as they are holdovers from yesterday, but the 7th-chord shape will take some time to get accustomed to. Notice, however, that the 7th-chord shape used in the exercises differs from the one shown in the diagrams (the high E string has been eliminated). The reason for this is because the riff that we'll be working on in the next section omits this note, so it makes sense to practice the voicing this way. At the same time, it's good to familiarize yourself with the complete voicing that the shape is based on.

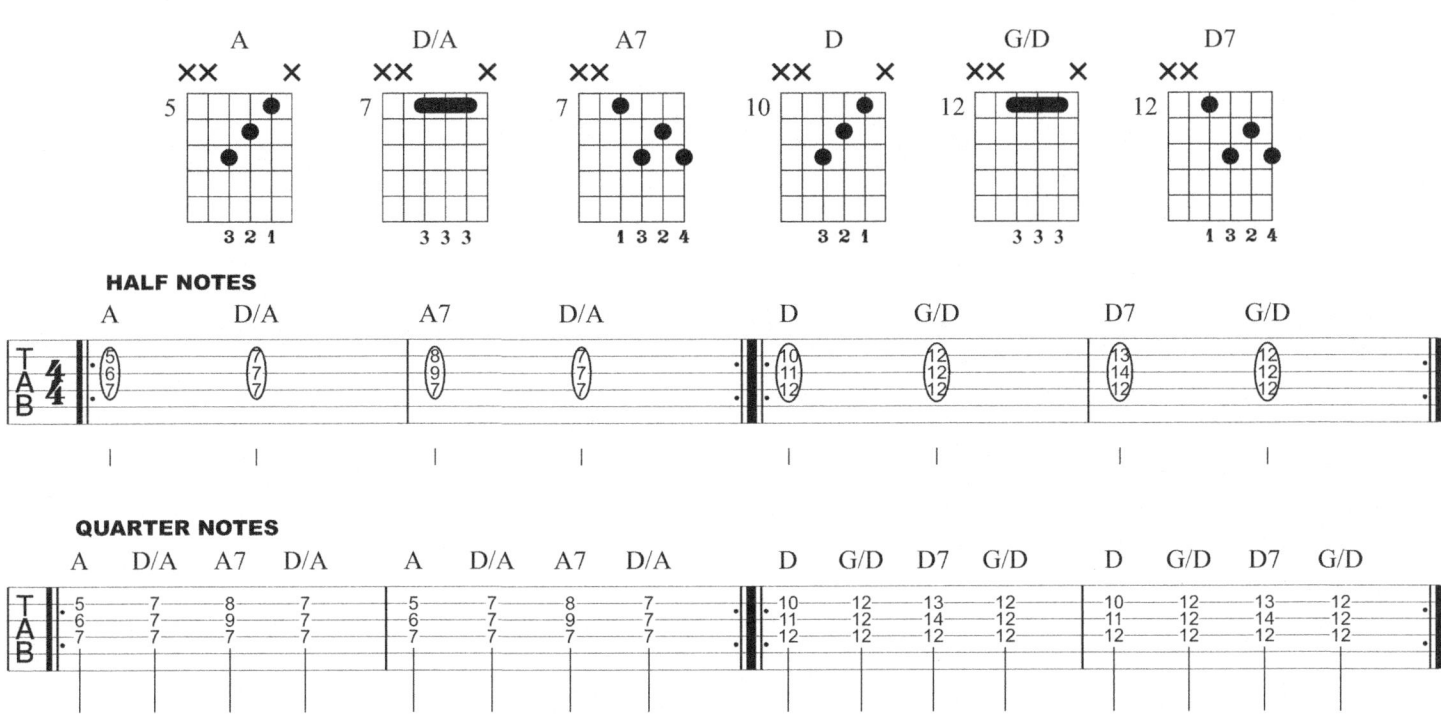

RHYTHM & HARMONY (1:15–1:00)

This riff is an extension of the one from yesterday. Again, use a combination of your pick (string 4) and middle and ring fingers (strings 3–2) to pluck the strings. Also, you might want to experiment with your frethand fingerings for this one. You might find that an index-finger barre is more efficient than a ring-finger barre at the seventh and 12th frets.

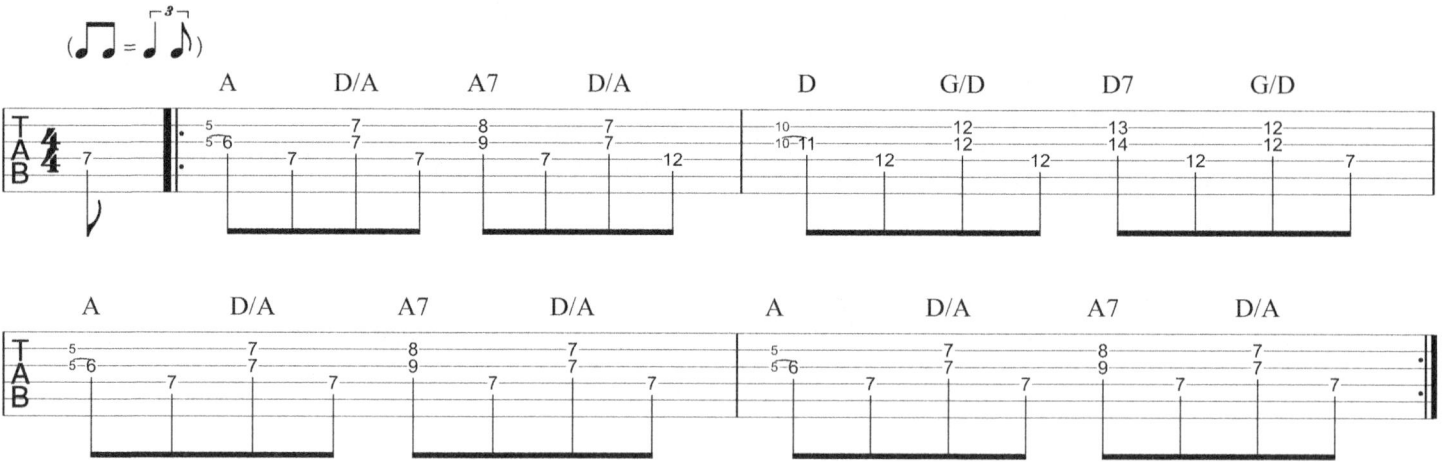

SCALE (1:00–0:45)

Here's the A major pentatonic scale from yesterday arranged in the upper octave. The fingerings are exactly the same and the root notes are located at the same fret/string locations. Use alternate (down-up) picking throughout, starting with a downstoke. Once you're comfortable with this, try starting with an upstroke.

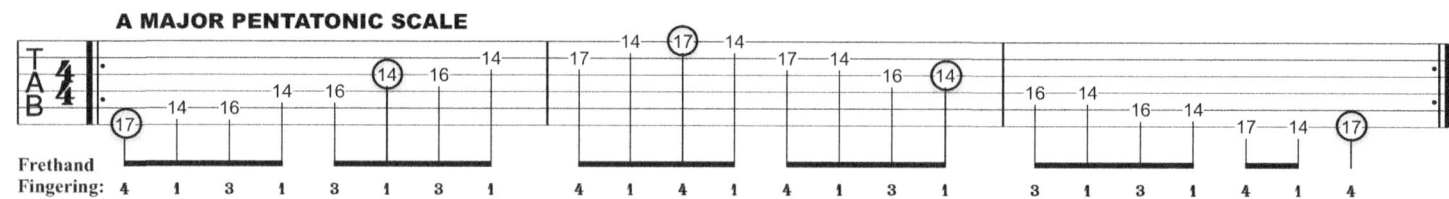

TECHNIQUE (0:45–0:30)

As a technique, it often takes a backseat to bends, hammer-ons, pull-offs, and slides, among others, but perhaps no technique is a vital to the blues as vibrato. In fact, it's the one technique that really gives a guitarist his or her identity as a player.

Vibrato is a rapid variation in pitch. On guitar, we produce vibrato by rapidly pushing or pulling a string slightly sharp and then back to its original pitch (classical guitarists achieve this by rapidly rolling a frethand finger back and forth horizontally on the string). Vibrato is crucial to the sound of blues guitar, as exemplified by the late B.B. King and Stevie Ray Vaughan. The two examples below feature the upper-octave A major pentatonic scale, played first in ascending fashion with vibrato placed on every other note. In the second example, the scale is descended and vibrato is placed on the notes that didn't receive it in exercise 1.

LEAD LICK (0:30–0:15)

This four-bar lick is played over the double-stop riff from the Rhythm & Harmony section. It features several of the techniques we've been working on, including whole-step bends, hammer-ons, pull-offs, and vibrato. Check out the audio to hear how the line sounds over the A–D–A (I–IV–I) progression, then try playing it yourself (several times!).

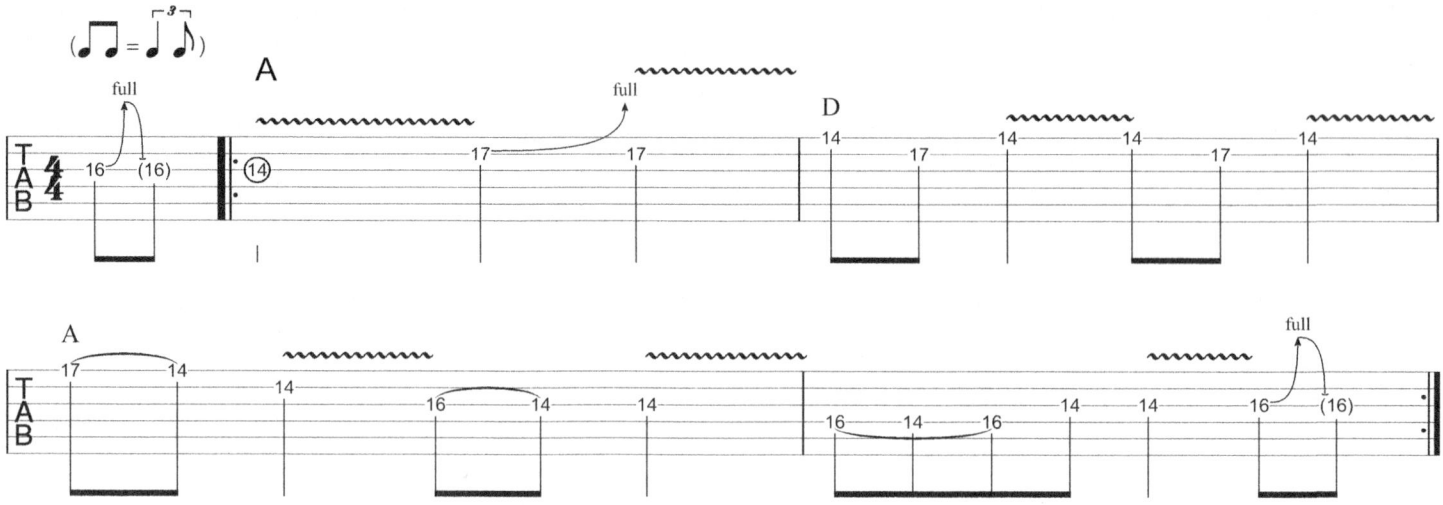

TURNAROUND (0:15–0:00)

This turnaround is a bit more challenging than the ones we've learned up to this point due to the way it has to be fingered. With your pinky planted on fret 5 of string 1, use a combination of your ring, middle, and index fingers to descend string 4 (see the fingering below the tab staff). In measure 2, the walk up to the root of the V (E) chord occurs on the same string and culminates in a pared-down open-position E7 voicing.

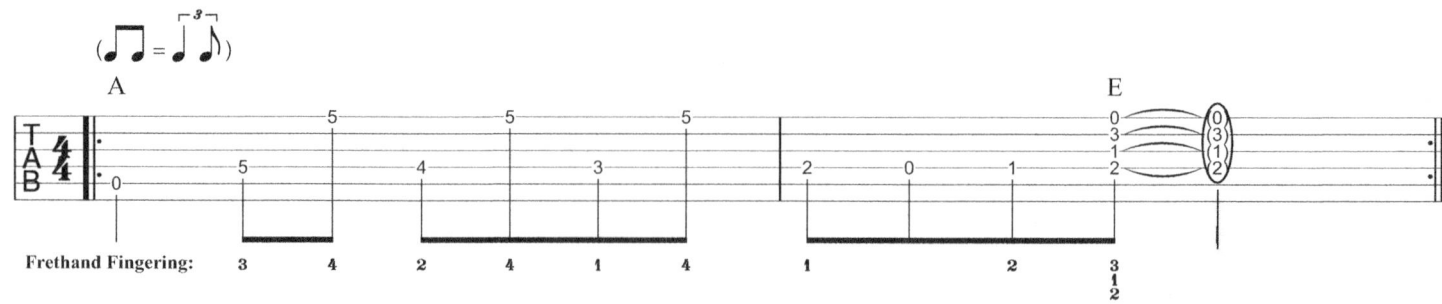

DAY 7

WEEK 1 REVIEW: PUTTING IT ALL TOGETHER (1:30–0:00)

Today is the culmination of a week's worth of hard work. For the next 90 minutes, we're going to practice the 12-bar solo that's notated below. The rhythm figure on the bottom tab staff should look familiar, as it's the riff that we learned yesterday. It's been notated here to show you how the riff is played over the entire 12-bar form, which includes all three changes—I (A), IV (D), and V (E). The turnaround should also look familiar, as it's the one we learned on Day 5. If you have another guitar player handy, they can play the rhythm part as you practice the solo.

The lead contains all of the techniques that we've learned up to this point—whole-step bends and pre-bends, hammer-ons, pull-offs, slides, and vibrato—and two of the scales, A blues and A major pentatonic. You've got plenty of practice time, so take it slow and try to minimize mistakes. As always, don't worry about memorizing all 12 bars; instead, focus on getting the proper feel and executing the techniques with authenticity. The licks that feel most natural to you will likely be the ones you end up incorporating into your own arsenal of licks.

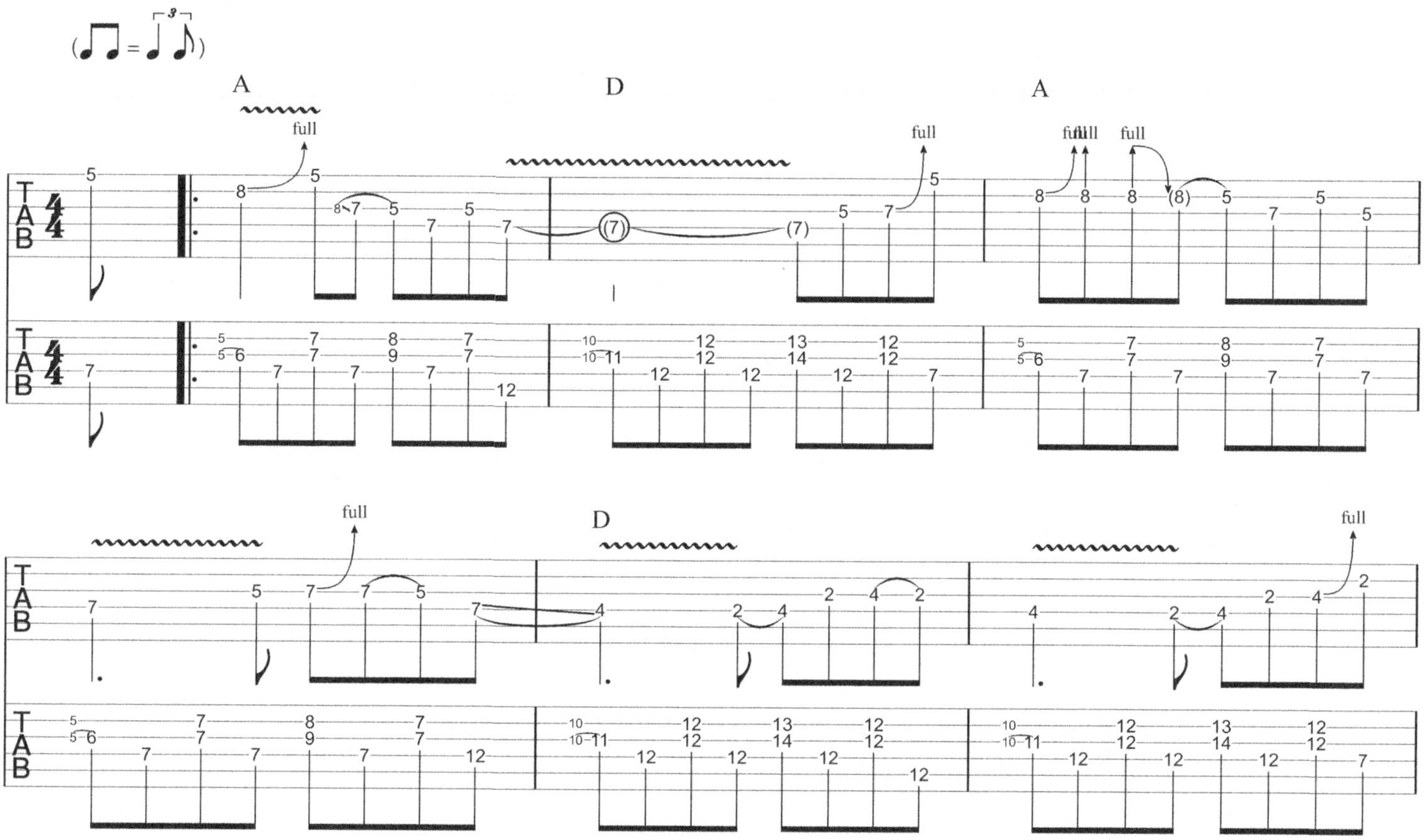

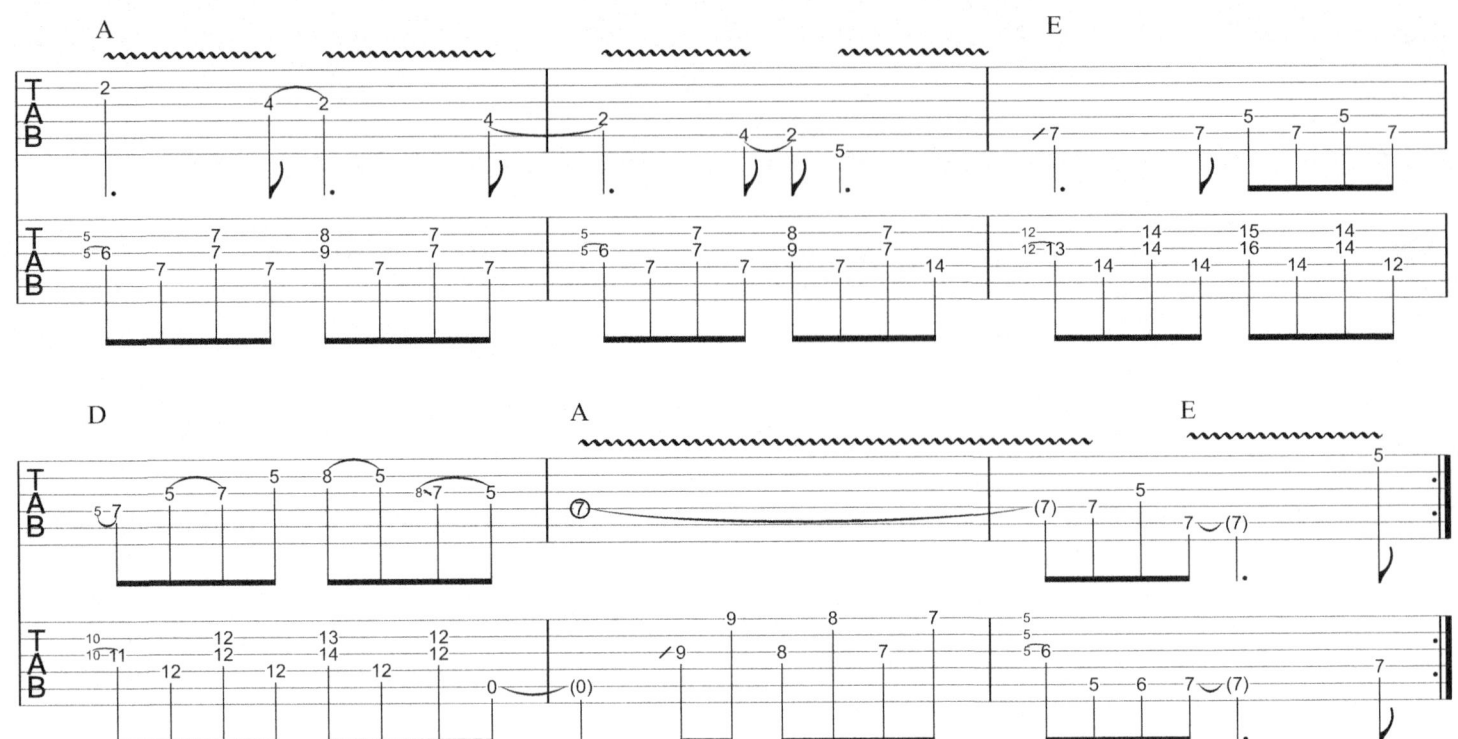

WEEK 2
DAY 8

CHORDS (1:30–1:15)

Our chordal focus today is on two forms of dominant 7th barre chords. Specifically, we're going to practice A7 and D7 voicings whose roots are located on strings 6 and 5, respectively. But, as with all barre chords, these shapes can be moved up or down the fretboard to change keys. Rhythmically, we're going start by playing the chords in half notes, then move on to quarter notes. When changing from A7 to D7, leave your index finger barred across all six strings. This will make the change more efficient and eliminate unwanted string noise.

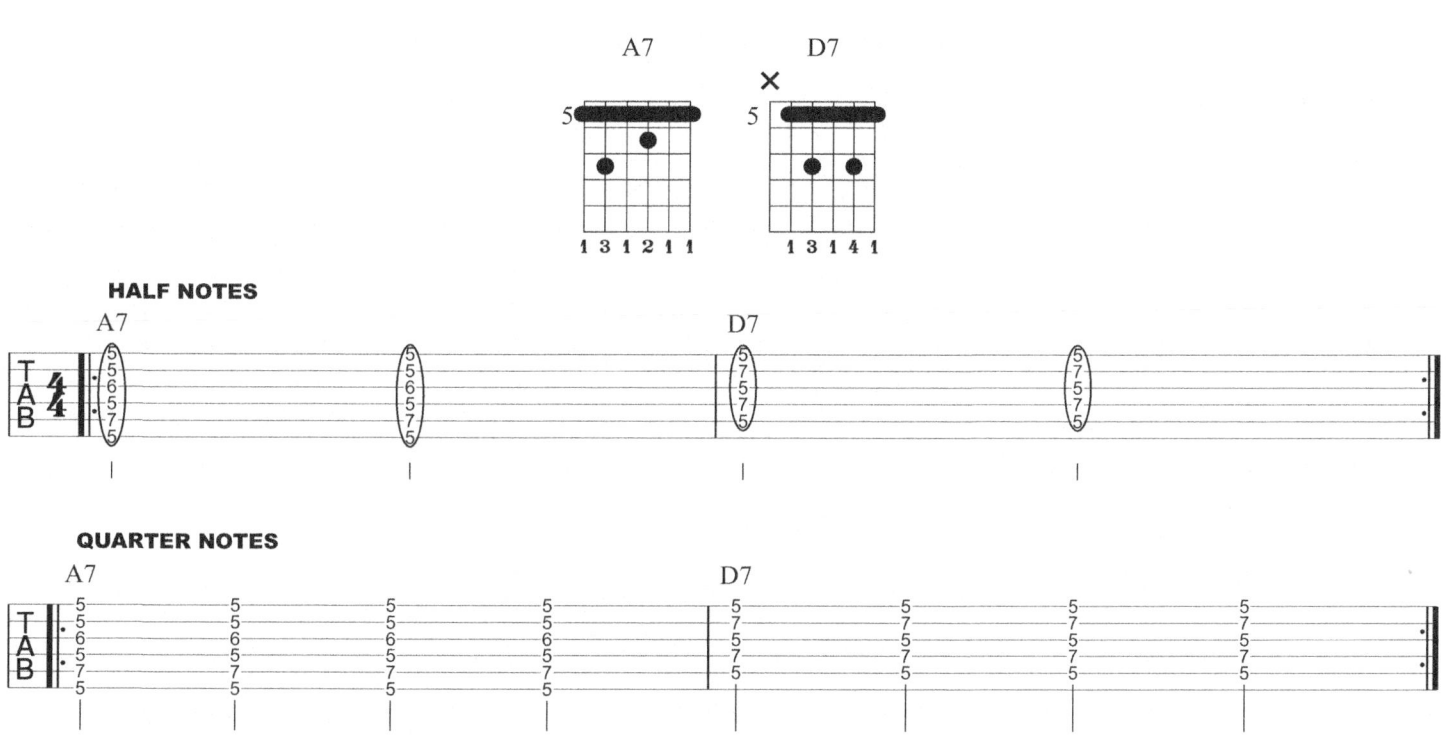

RHYTHM & HARMONY (1:15–1:00)

This riff is based on rhumba-style blues. The main characteristics of rhumba blues are straight (not swung) eighth notes and silence (rest) on beat 2 of each measure, with the riff's second note coming on the "and" (upbeat) of beat 2. You'll notice that the 7th chords are carryovers from our previous section. The challenge here is moving between the chord strums and the single-note lines, which are derived from the A major and D major pentatonic scales.

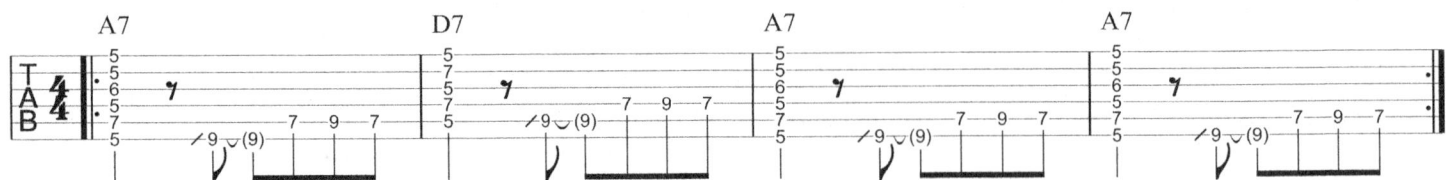

SCALE (1:00–0:45)

We've already covered the blues scale, which, as we learned, is a minor scale. Now, we're going to turn our attention to the major-key version of that scale. Below is A major blues in second position. The only difference between this scale and its minor-key counterpart is where the root notes are located—the fingering is exactly the same. If you remember, we added the b5th (Bb) to turn the E minor pentatonic scale into the E blues scale. Here, we take the major pentatonic scale and add the b3rd (C), turning the A major pentatonic scale into the A major blues scale. The presence of the b3rd creates chromaticism between the 2nd/9th (B) and the major 3rd (C#), and this juxtaposition of the minor 3rd (b3rd) and major 3rd is a defining sound of the blues—one that we've seen in action in previous examples.

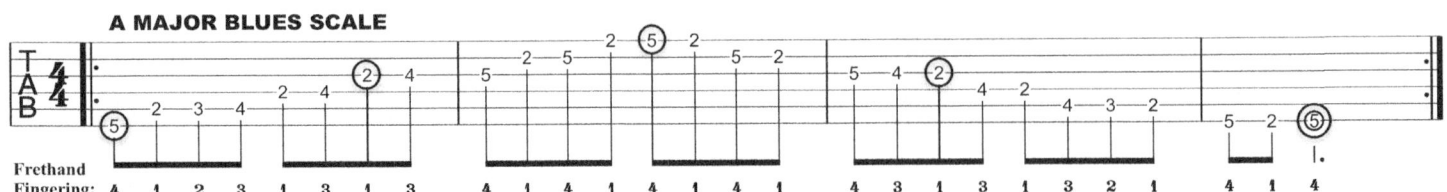

TECHNIQUE (0:45–0:30)

So far, our string bending has been relegated to the whole-step variety. Now it's time to turn our attention to some common half-step bends. As with whole-step bends, we're going to let our ears guide us to the target pitches. Each of the four examples below bend notes from the A major blues scale a half step to another pitch found inside the same scale. In exercises 1 and 3, we're bending the third-string B note (2nd/9th) a half step to the b3rd (C). In exercises 2 and 4, we're bending the fifth-string C note (b3rd) a half step to the major 3rd (C#). In the latter two examples, we're also releasing the bends back to their original pitches. Executing a half-step bend takes relatively little effort, so be sure not to over-bend and turn your half steps into whole steps!

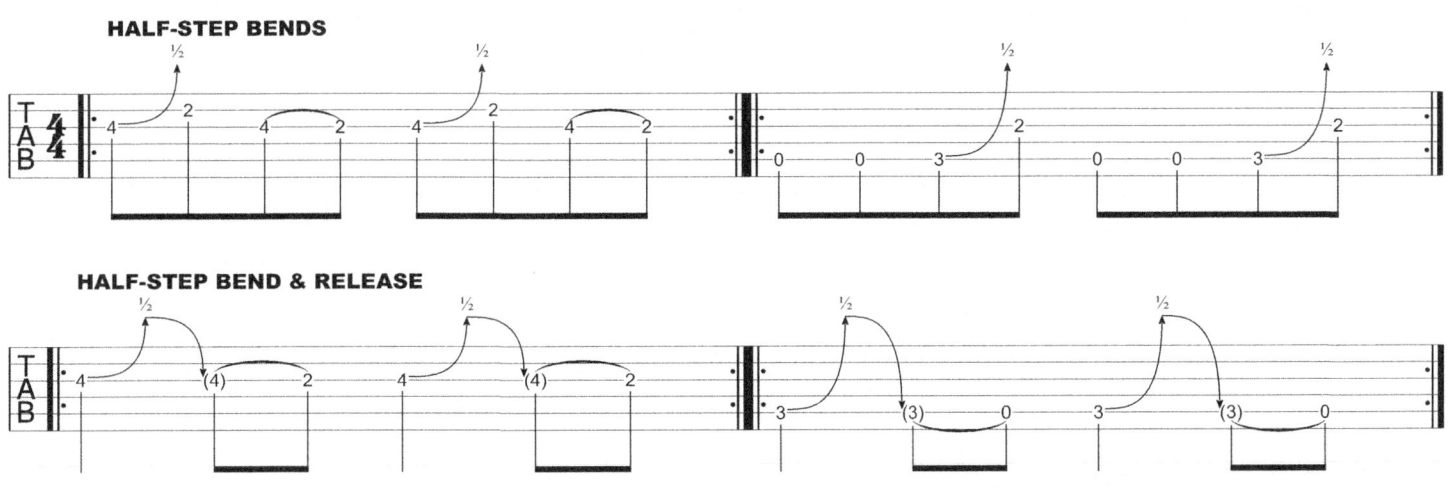

LEAD LICK (0:30–0:15)

This four-bar lick is played over the blues rhumba that we learned back in the Rhythm & Harmony section and features everything from half-step bends and slides to hammer-ons, pull-offs, and pre-bends. Since this is a rhumba, be sure to play the eighth notes straight rather than with a swing feel. And don't overlook the pickup measure, which has us coming in on the "and" (upbeat) of beat 2.

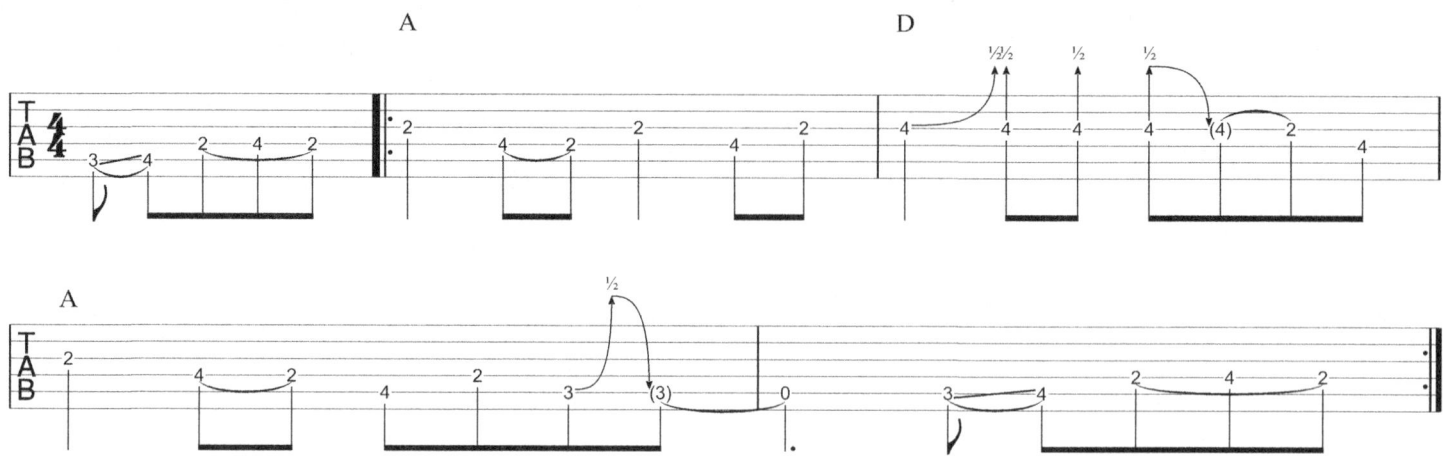

TURNAROUND (0:15–0:00)

This turnaround is a lot of fun to play, but it's also a bit tricky for the frethand. We're going to start by planting our pinky on fret 5 of string 1, using our middle and ring fingers for the notes on strings 4 and 2, respectively. Then, on beat 3 of measure 1, we're going to shift our middle and ring fingers down to fret 4 while leaving our pinky at fret 5. On beat 4, we're going to replace the middle and ring fingers with our index, using it to barre across strings 4–2. At the onset of measure 2, we'll shift the index finger down to fret 2 and wrap up the turnaround with an E7 chord that we've used previously.

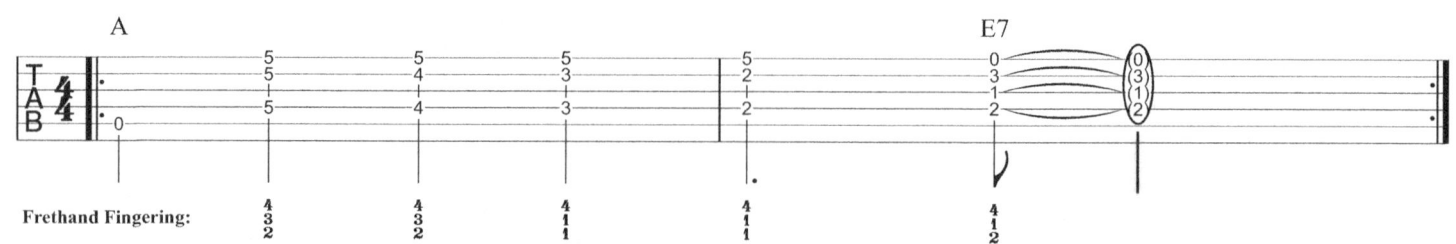

DAY 9

CHORDS (1:30–1:15)

Triads and seventh chords are not the only type of chords found in the blues. Nearly as common are ninth chords and, to a lesser degree, sixth chords. The exercises below feature popular voicings for each type, played as staccato quarter notes and then syncopated eighth notes. Play the staccato quarter notes short (don't let them ring out) and punchy. As for the syncopated eighth notes, play them exclusively on the upbeats. Since the eighth notes are swung in this exercise, this means the upbeat occurs a little later in the beat than if they were straight eighths. To get the proper feel, listen to the audio.

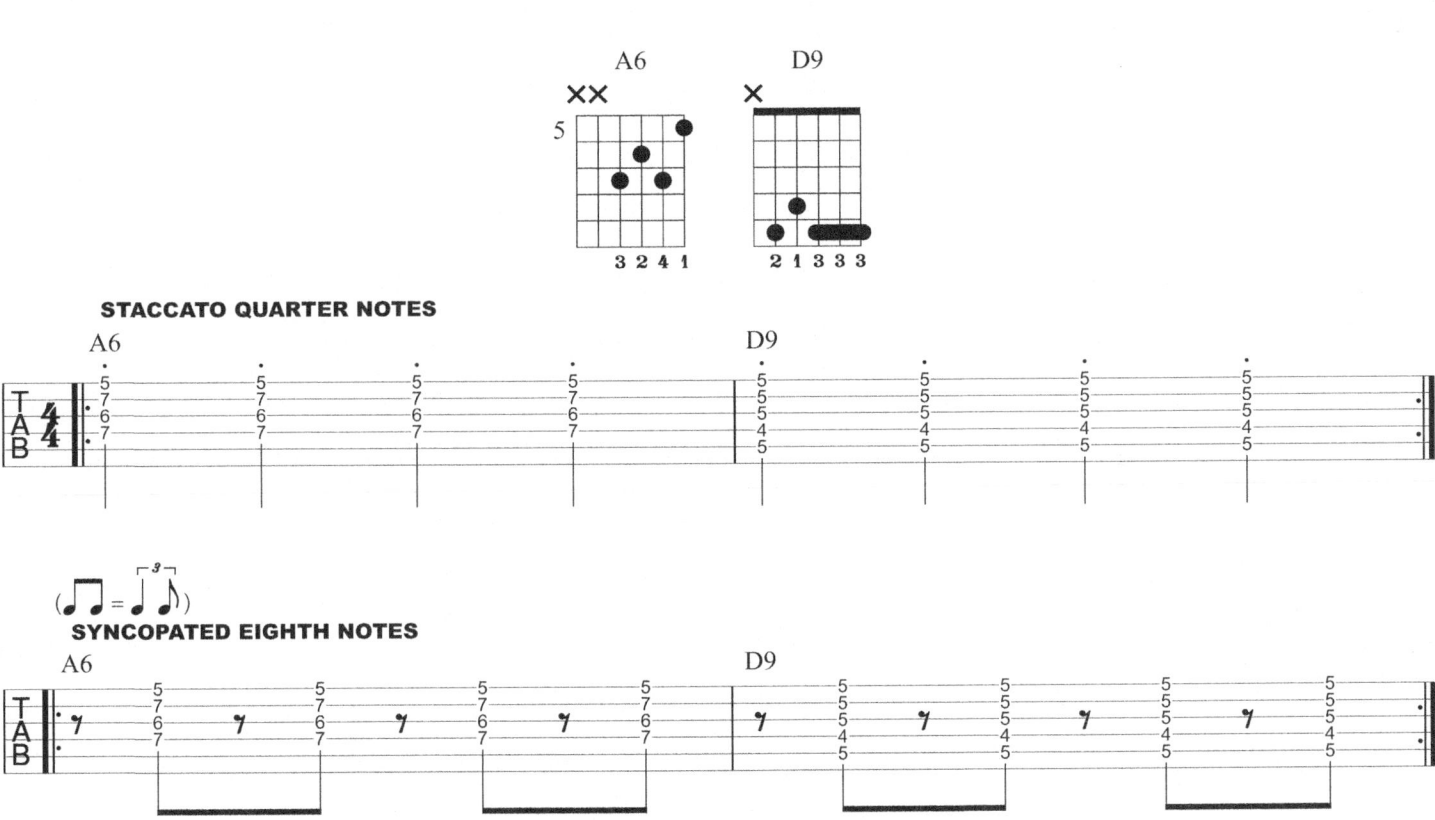

RHYTHM & HARMONY (1:15–1:00)

Now let's take the chord voicings that we just learned, A6 and D9, and apply them to a rhythm that is quite popular in jump blues (a.k.a., jazz blues or swing blues). The rhythm is a combination of the staccato quarter notes and syncopated eighth notes that we worked on in the previous section. One slight chordal variation occurs in measure 4, where we'll move our pinky up one fret on string 2 to briefly imply A7.

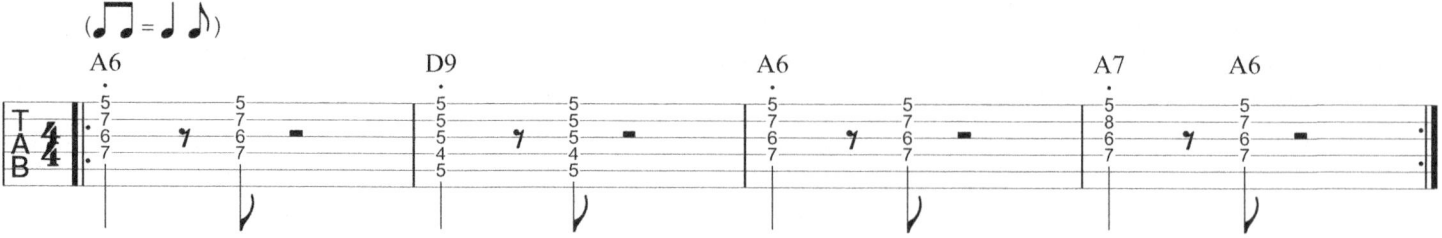

SCALE (1:00–0:45)

Here's the A major blues scale in the upper octave (14th position). Like all our scales, pay special attention to the locations of the root notes, as they act as "guideposts" when learning and using new scales. Practice the scale for the full 15 minutes, increasing your tempo only after you're able to play through it without making mistakes.

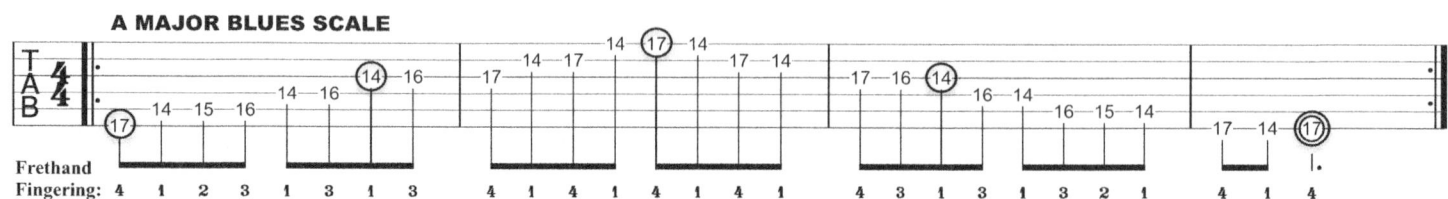

TECHNIQUE (0:45–0:30)

These four one-bar exercises feature some common—and some not-so-common—half-step pre-bends and releases. The first two exercises involve bending and pre-bending the B note at fret 16 of string 3 up a half step to C, the b3rd. Exercises 3 and 4 feature the same bends, only they're played an octave lower (on string 5). Bass-string bends are not as common as treble-string bends, but they're good to have at your disposal nonetheless. Bend with your ring finger (reinforced with your middle and index) in exercises 1 and 2, and your index finger in exercises 3 and 4.

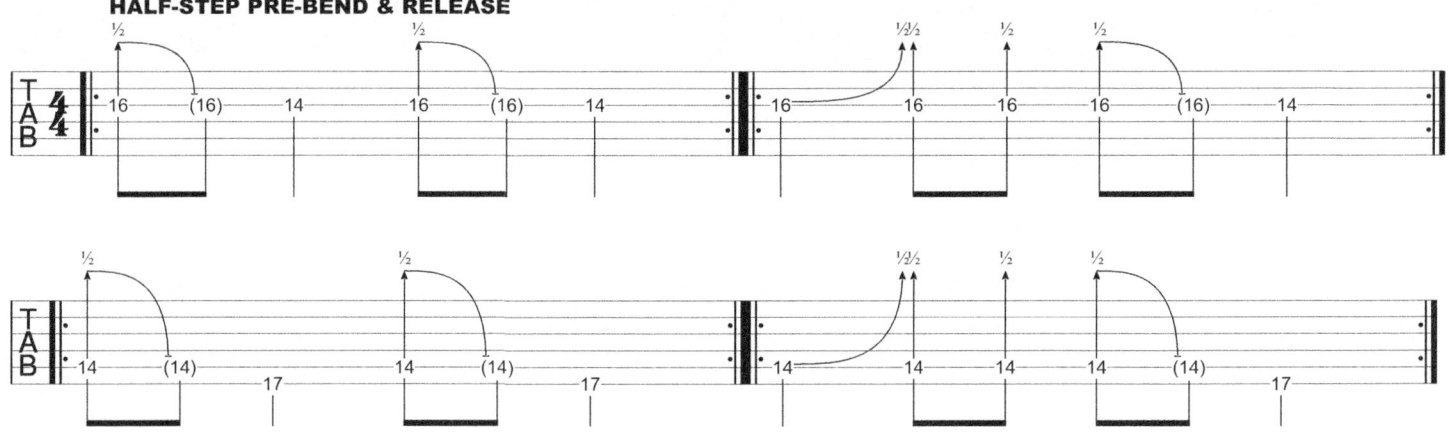

LEAD LICK (0:30–0:15)

The A major blues scale provides the pitches for this four-bar jump blues lick. The pre-bends in bar 1 are restated an octave lower (on string 5) in bar 2. When the line reaches string 6 in bar 3, it reverses course and works its way up to the root note on string 3 for resolution.

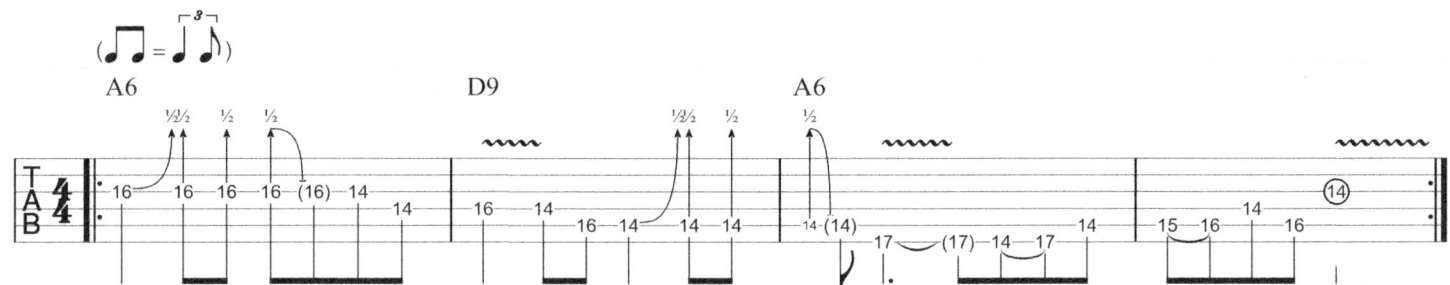

TURNAROUND (0:15–0:00)

We first encountered this progression, I–IV–I–V, on Day 3, only here it's played in the key of A. The jump-blues rhythm pattern introduced in the Rhythm & Harmony section is the rhythmic foundation of this turnaround, which features nifty half-step movement to the V chord: F9–E9.

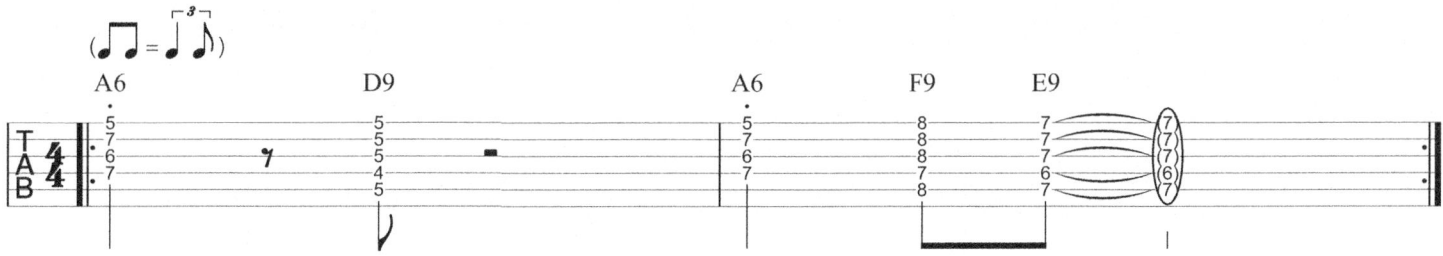

DAY 10

CHORDS (1:30–1:15)

We have one new chord to learn today, A9, which is voiced on strings 4–1. The E9, on the other hand, is the same voicing as the D9 chord from yesterday, only played two frets higher up the neck. If this A9 voicing is new to you, spend some extra time getting acquainted with it before moving on to the exercises. It's a bit awkward at first, but once you have it, you'll be able to move in and out of it with ease.

All three exercises move from E9 to A9, rhythmically starting with eighth notes before moving on to 16th notes and some syncopation. Count the 16th notes as follows: "1-ee-&-uh, 2-ee-&-uh, 3-ee-&-uh, 4-ee-&-uh," etc. The dotted eighth/16th note grouping is counted the same way, although you'll hold the dotted eighth through the first three 16ths ("1-ee-&"), playing the last (fourth) 16th note on the "uh." As always, listen to the audio to hear how they should be played.

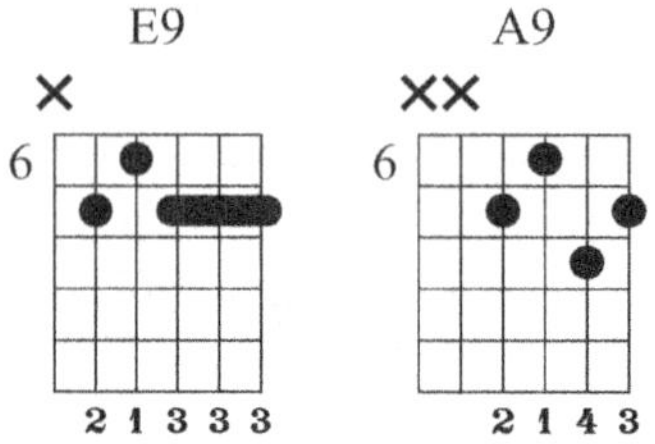

EIGHTH NOTES

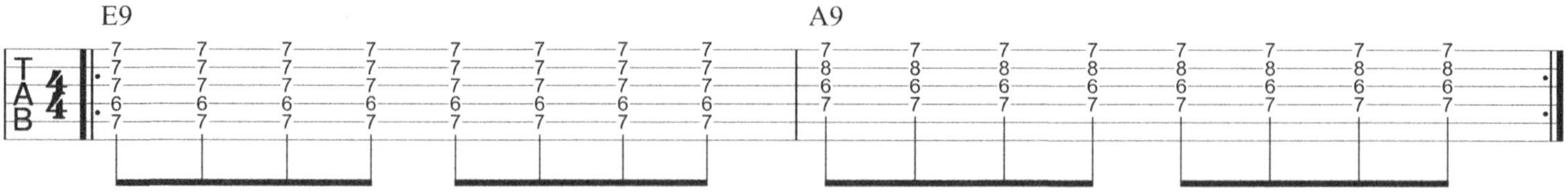

16TH NOTES

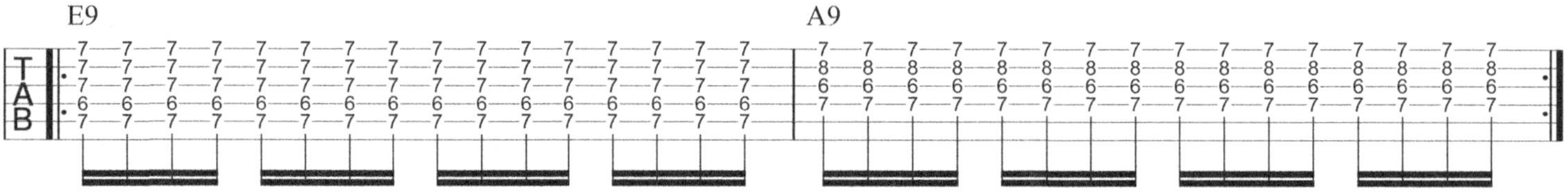

DOTTED EIGHTH NOTES

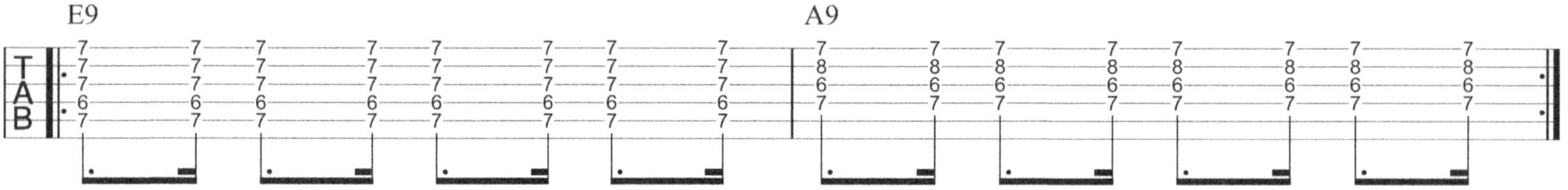

RHYTHM & HARMONY (1:15–1:00)

Now we're going to put our E9 and A9 voicings to work. This example is a funk blues played over the first six bars of a 12-bar blues. After a syncopated chord strum on beat 1, a single-note line derived from the E minor pentatonic scale comes in on the "and" of beat 2 and finishes out the measure. This pattern is repeated throughout, with the chords changing from E9 to A9 at bar 5. At this point, the scale notes change from E minor to A minor pentatonic, as well.

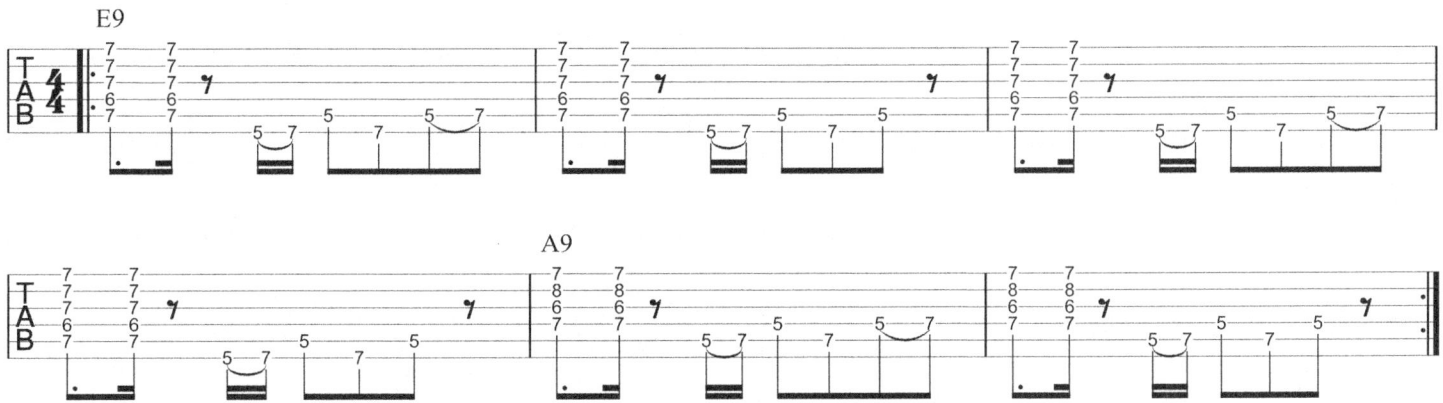

SCALE (1:00–0:45)

Up to this point, our focus has been on five-note pentatonic scales and their six-note counterparts, the blues scale. Here, we're going to learn our first seven-note scale, E Dorian. Technically, Dorian is not a scale; instead, it's a "mode" of the major scale. We could start on any one of the major scale's seven pitches and play a different mode. In this case, E Dorian is the second mode of the D major scale (D–E–F#–G–A–B–C#)—meaning, they share the exact same pitches but their roots are different. Dorian is one of a few modes favored by blues guitarists, so be sure to get to know it intimately.

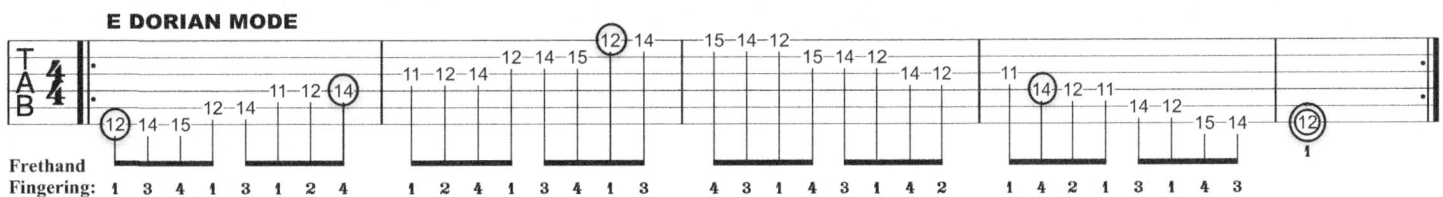

TECHNIQUE (0:45–0:30)

In the blues, quarter-step bends are nearly as common as half- and whole-step bends. Quarter steps are located half way between two pitches that are separated by a semitone (half step). Since we can't fret these "microtones" on the guitar, we have to use bends to achieve these pitches. Bend upward with either your ring finger or pinky in exercise 1, and bend downward with your index finger in exercise 2.

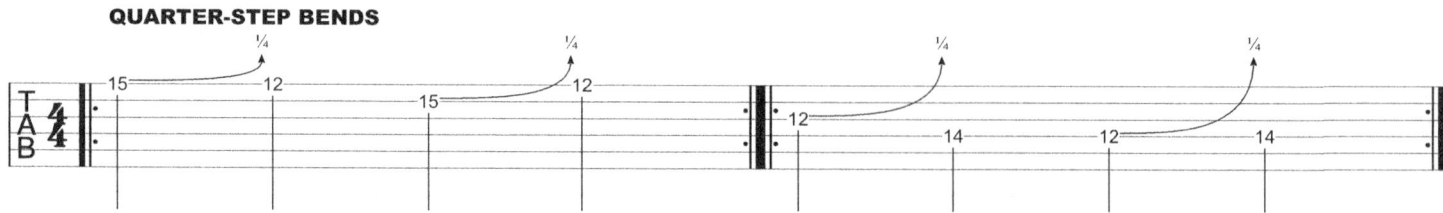

LEAD LICK (0:30–0:15)

This entire lick is rooted in the E Dorian mode and prominently features quarter- and half-step bends, as well as hammer-ons, pull-offs, and vibrato. Additionally, melodic motifs play a strong role in the overall sound of the phrase: a one-bar motif is created in measure 1 and then answered in measure 2, and similar strategies are used in measures 3–4 (half-step bends) and measures 5–6 (half-note vibrato and eighth notes).

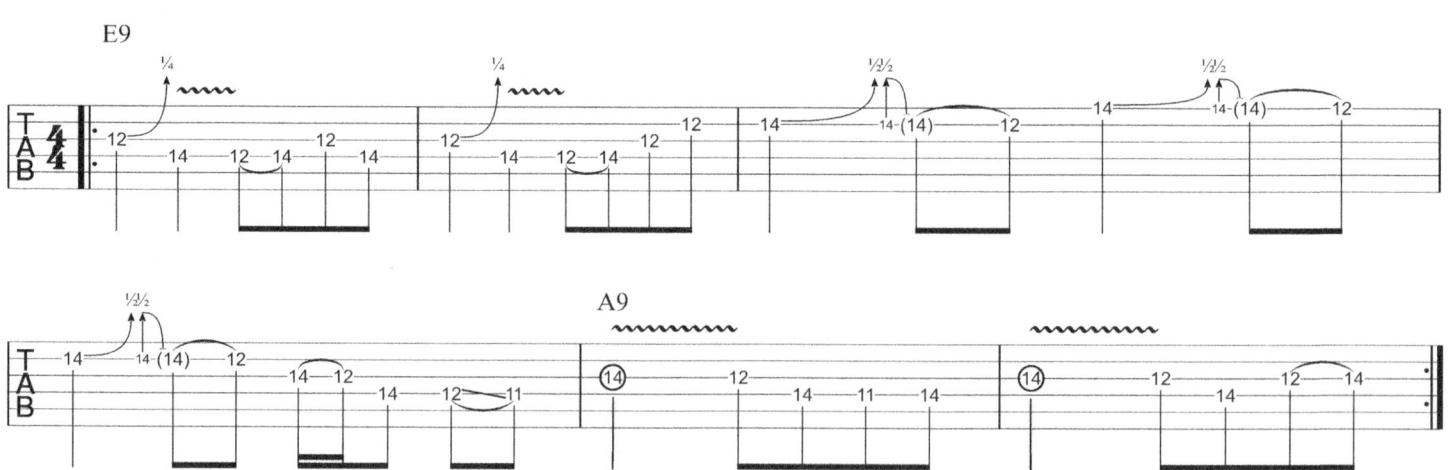

TURNAROUND (0:15–0:00)

Here's the familiar I–IV–I–V progression making another appearance in one of our turnarounds. You should already be familiar with the ninth chords, as they are the voicings we used in our funk blues rhythm figure. The B7#5 chord, however, is brand new. To voice this chord, we'll place our index finger on string 6 (at fret 7), our middle finger on string 4 (fret 7), our ring finger on string 3 (fret 8), and our pinky on string 2 (fret 8). Be sure to flatten your index finger just enough to come into contact with and mute string 5.

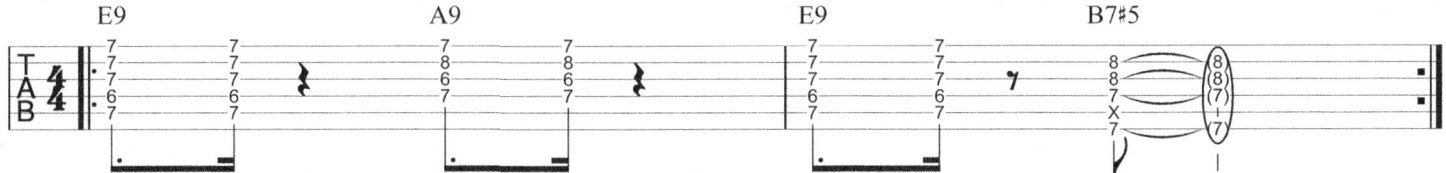

DAY 11

CHORDS (1:30–1:15)

Today, we're going to learn a new ninth-chord voicing. Played here as A9, this voicing has as nice, open sound and works well with the ninth-chord voicing that we already know. Below are a couple of exercises in 12/8 time. If you're unfamiliar with 12/8, this meter has 12 beats per measure, with eighth notes receiving the beat. Listen to the accompanying audio to hear the examples in action. The first one is a relatively easy straight-eighths exercise, while the second one is a shuffle rhythm.

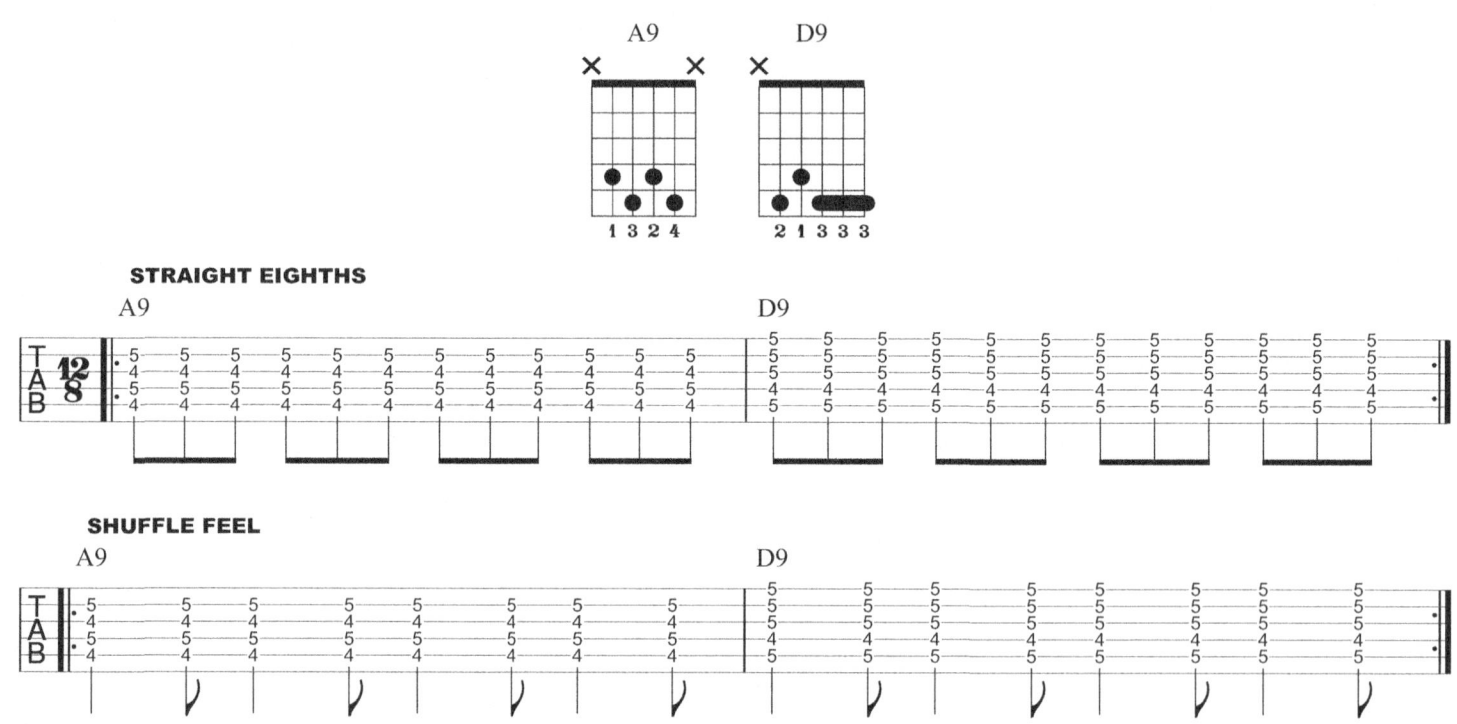

RHYTHM & HARMONY (1:15–1:00)

This rhythm figure features a technique that's popular amongst guitar players when playing over a slow blues: sliding 9ths. The chord fragments below are based on the A9 and D9 chords we learned in the previous section; however, the fingering for A9 has to be adjusted in order to incorporate the root, A, which is absent from the voicing we learned. Wrap your thumb over the top of the neck to fret string 6 at fret 5, using your middle, index, and ring fingers to fret strings 4–2, respectively. After plucking string 6, release your thumb so you can perform the chordal slide. Use the same technique for the D9 chord, releasing your middle finger from string 5 so the slide can be executed with the ring finger.

42

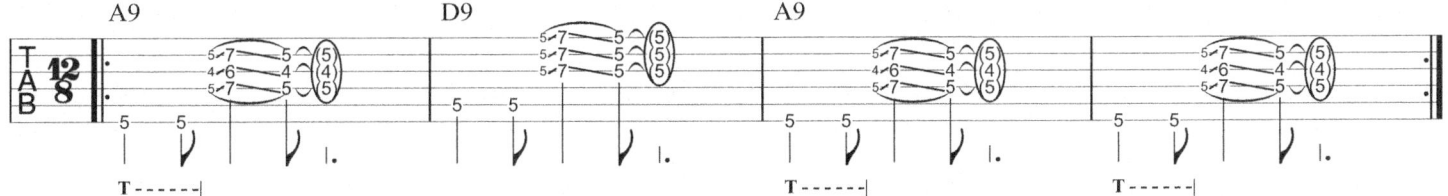

SCALE (1:00–0:45)

Yesterday, we learned our first mode, and today we're going to learn our second, A Mixolydian. The Mixolydian mode is the fifth mode of the major scale and is a great choice for soloing over dominant seventh chords. Without getting too deep into music theory, the reason for this is the fact that, like dominant seventh chords, the Mixolydian mode has both a major 3rd and a minor 7th—intervals that define the blues sound.

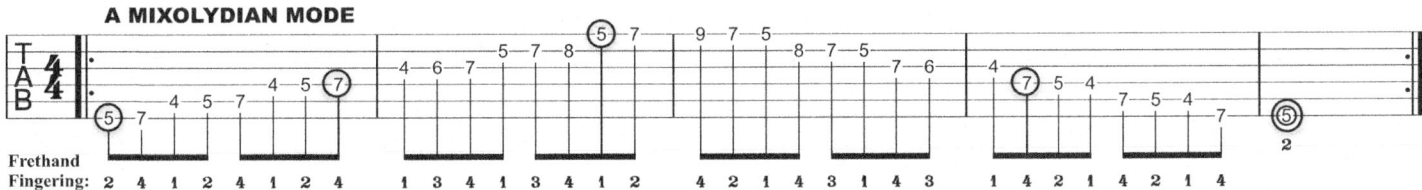

TECHNIQUE (0:45–0:30)

We've touched on double stops and sliding chord partials in previous sections, but here we're going to look at how double stops, or "dyads," can be specifically applied to the A Mixolydian mode. In exercise 1, double-stop hammer-ons and slides are applied to string pairs 1–2, 2–3, and 3–4. Then, in exercise 2, a similar approach is taken, only slides are used exclusively.

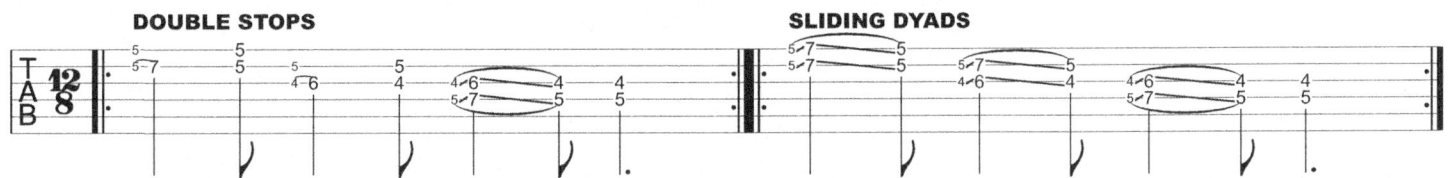

LEAD LICK (0:30–0:15)

This four-bar phrase, rooted entirely in A Mixolydian, is played over the sliding-ninths rhythm figure from earlier. After a half bar of silence (rest), the line launches into a pair of double stops. In measure 2, the D9 chord is outlined with both single notes and sliding dyads. This is followed in measure 3 by a repetitive four-note phrase that gives way to a descending line in measure 4 that resolves to the A note at fret 5 of string 6.

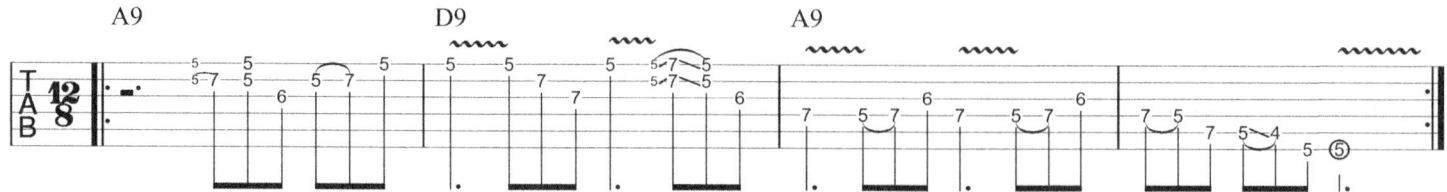

TURNAROUND (0:15–0:00)

This turnaround phrase is a lot of fun to play. It starts with the open A string, which is followed by a single-note line that juxtaposes the A note at fret 7 of string 4 and a chromatically ascending line on string 5. Be sure to play attention to the fingering indicated below the tab staff, as this is the most efficient way to voice the line. In measure 2, the double stop on beat 1 is followed by a half-step F9-to-E9 chord maneuver that signals it's time to go back to the top of the 12-bar form.

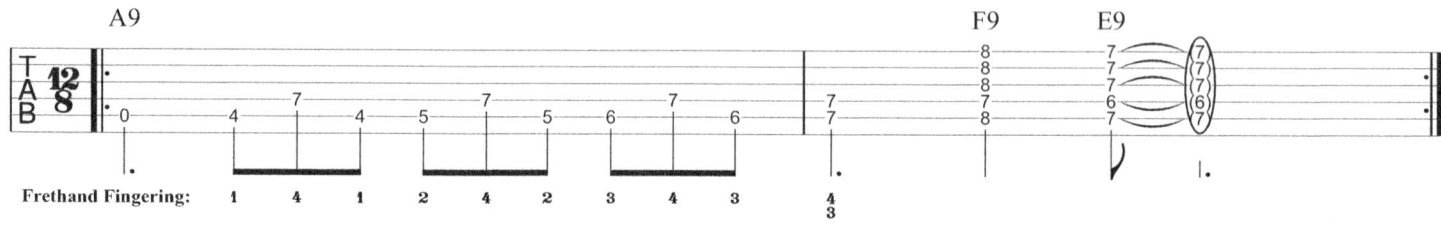

DAY 12

CHORDS (1:30–1:15)

Today, we're going to take our first look at minor blues. Before we get to the progressions, licks, and turnarounds, we need to familiarize ourselves with the chords. Below are some common minor seventh barre-chord shapes, played here as Am7 and Dm7. Sticking with the 12/8 meter from yesterday, exercise 1 features dotted quarter notes, which are played like regular quarter notes in 4/4 time. In exercise 2, the rhythm changes to straight eighth notes, which look like eighth-note triplets in 4/4 time (same concept!).

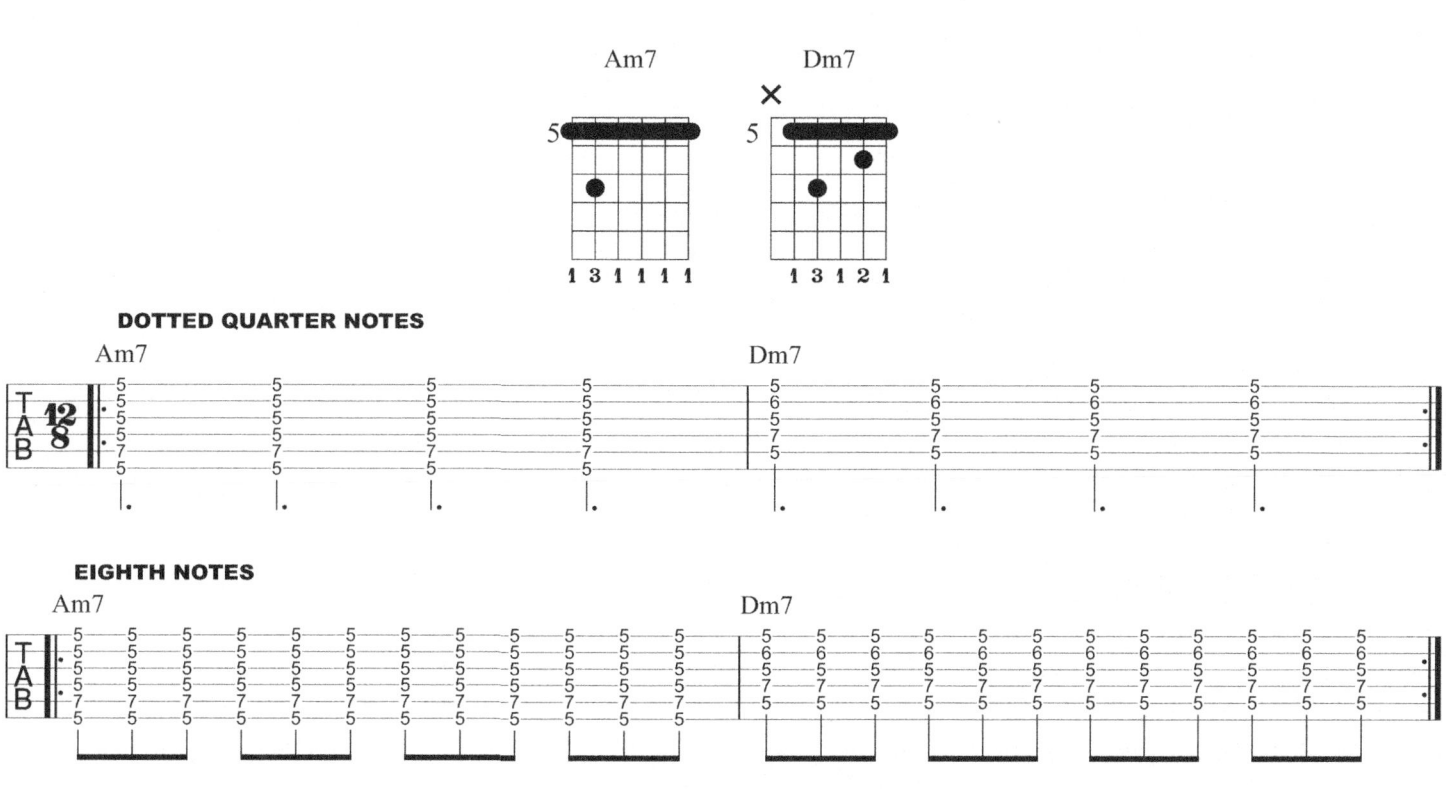

RHYTHM & HARMONY (1:15–1:00)

Below are the first four bars of a 12-bar minor blues in 12/8, with the iv (Dm7) chord appearing in bar 2 like previous examples. The rhythm is a bit different from the straight eighths in the previous section. Here, 16th notes appear on the second and eighth beat of each measure. Here's one way to count this: "1, 2-and, 3, 4, 5, 6, 7, 8-and, 9, 10, 11, 12," etc. If that's a tongue-twister, you can cut it in half: "1, 2-and, 3, 4, 5, 6." Then, you'd just count it twice for each measure.

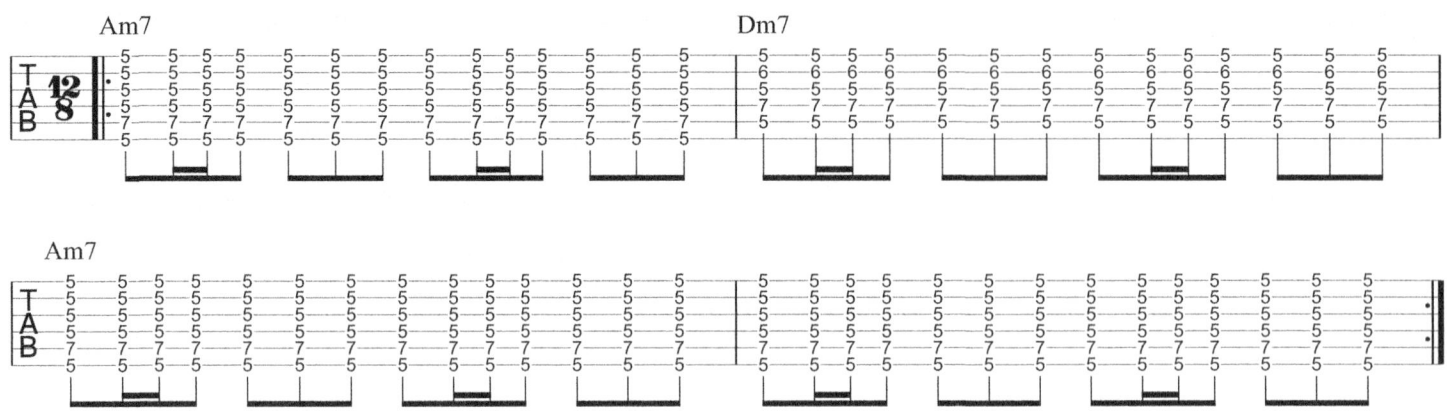

SCALE (1:00–0:45)

So far, we've tackled the Dorian and Mixolydian modes. Today, we're going to shift our focus to another seven-note mode, Aeolian, which is also known as the "natural minor scale," or simply the "minor scale." When we talk about minor keys or minor progressions, this is the scale they're based on. Although not as common as the minor pentatonic or blues scales, the natural minor scale is a good option for soloing over a minor blues progression. Again, be sure to pay close attention to where the root notes appear on the fretboard and within the scale pattern.

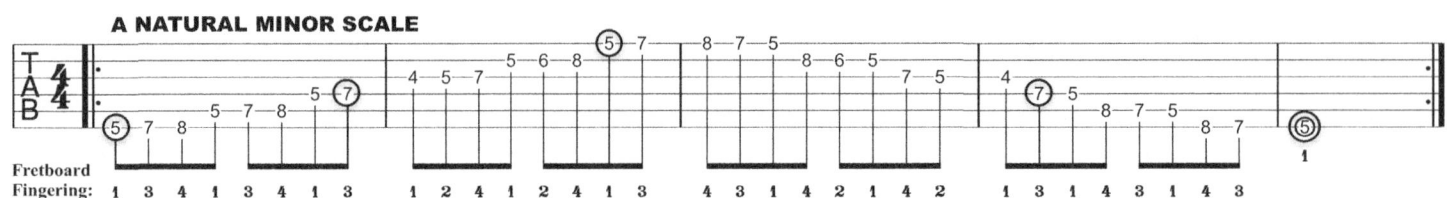

TECHNIQUE (0:45–0:30)

As a technique, string skipping often gets overshadowed by string bending, vibrato, and slides, among others, but it's a vital guitar technique nonetheless. If we were relegated to playing notes only on adjacent strings, our solos would get pretty stale—fast! The two exercises below feature four-note string-skipping sequences that descend (exercise 1) and ascend (exercise 2) the A natural minor scale. You'll notice that hammer-ons and pull-offs really come in handy when skipping strings, as they enable us to quickly reposition our pick to a non-adjacent string.

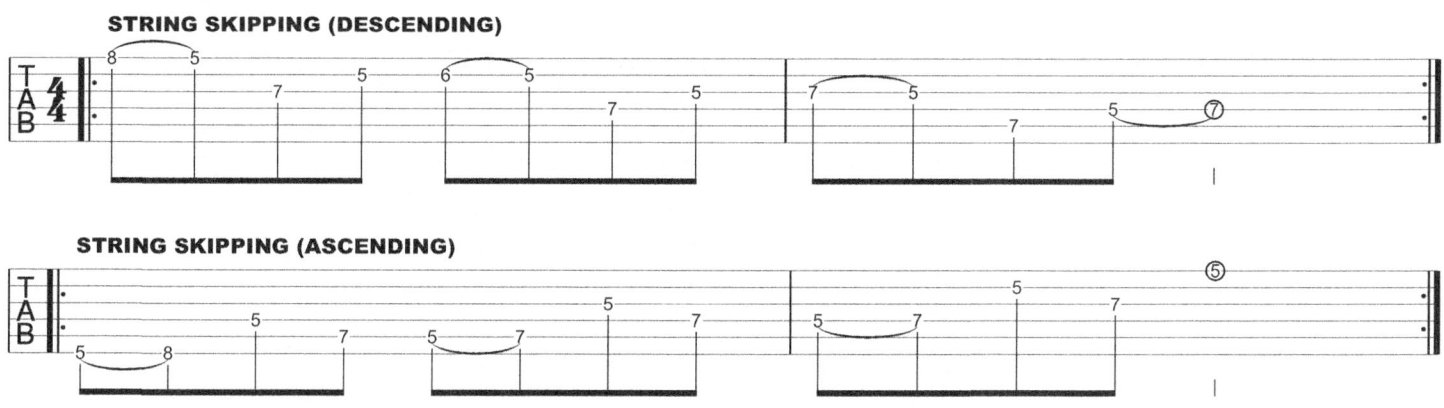

LEAD LICK (0:30–0:15)

This four-bar phrase, played over our Am7–Dm7–Am7 progression from earlier, features a plethora of techniques that we've learned over the past two weeks, including bends, hammer-ons, pull-offs, and string skipping. This lick is a good example of how to make a seven-note scale—in this case, A natural minor—sound bluesy, almost like its five-note counterpart, A minor pentatonic.

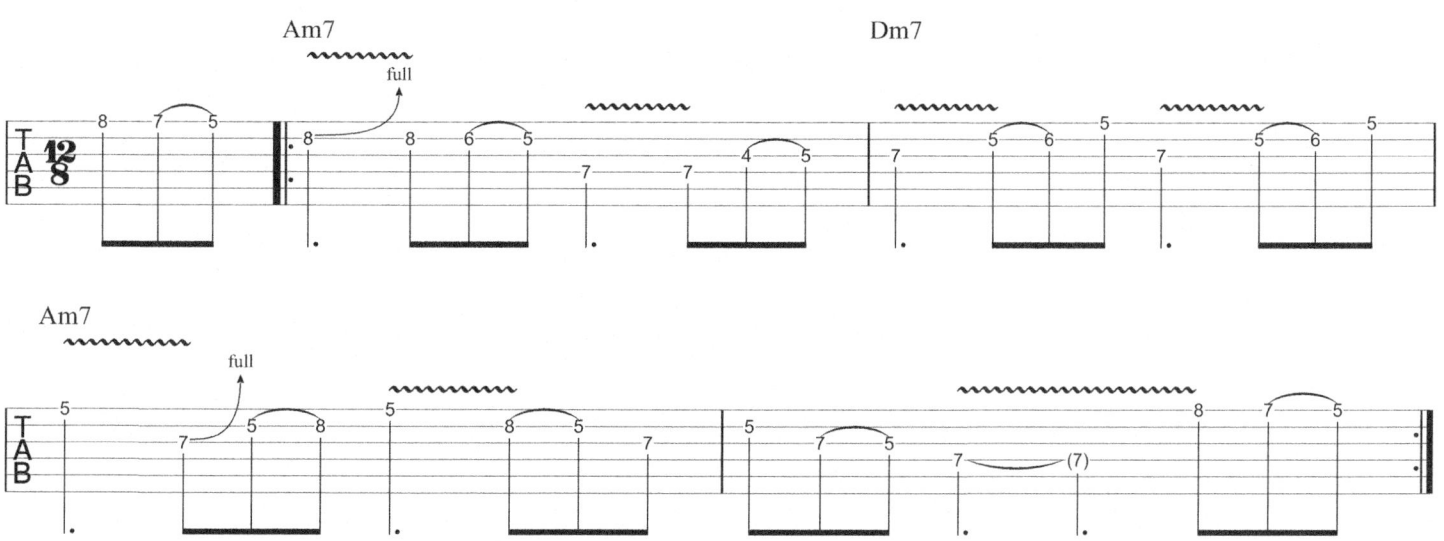

TURNAROUND (0:15–0:00)

The progression in this turnaround should look familiar, as it's the trusty I–IV–I–V changes that we've used several times over the past two weeks. The difference here, though, is that it's in a minor key (A minor), with each chord voiced as a minor seventh barre chord, giving us an Am7–Dm7–Am7–Em7 (i7–iv7–i7–v7) progression.

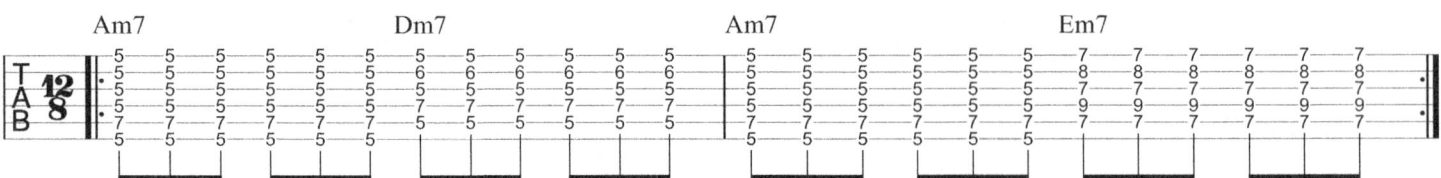

DAY 13

CHORDS (1:30–1:15)

This set of chords is a variation on the one used in yesterday's turnaround. Here, we have a new (and very cool-sounding) Am7, and in place of Em7, we have E7#9—the "Hendrix chord." The Am7-to-Dm7 change is a bit trickier with this voicing, but it's a good chord to know and utilize. Also, spend some extra time getting acquainted with the E7#9 voicing. Once you have the voicings under your fingers, give the exercises a few passes. They start slowly with dotted half notes in exercise 1 and then pick up the pace with dotted quarter notes in exercise 2.

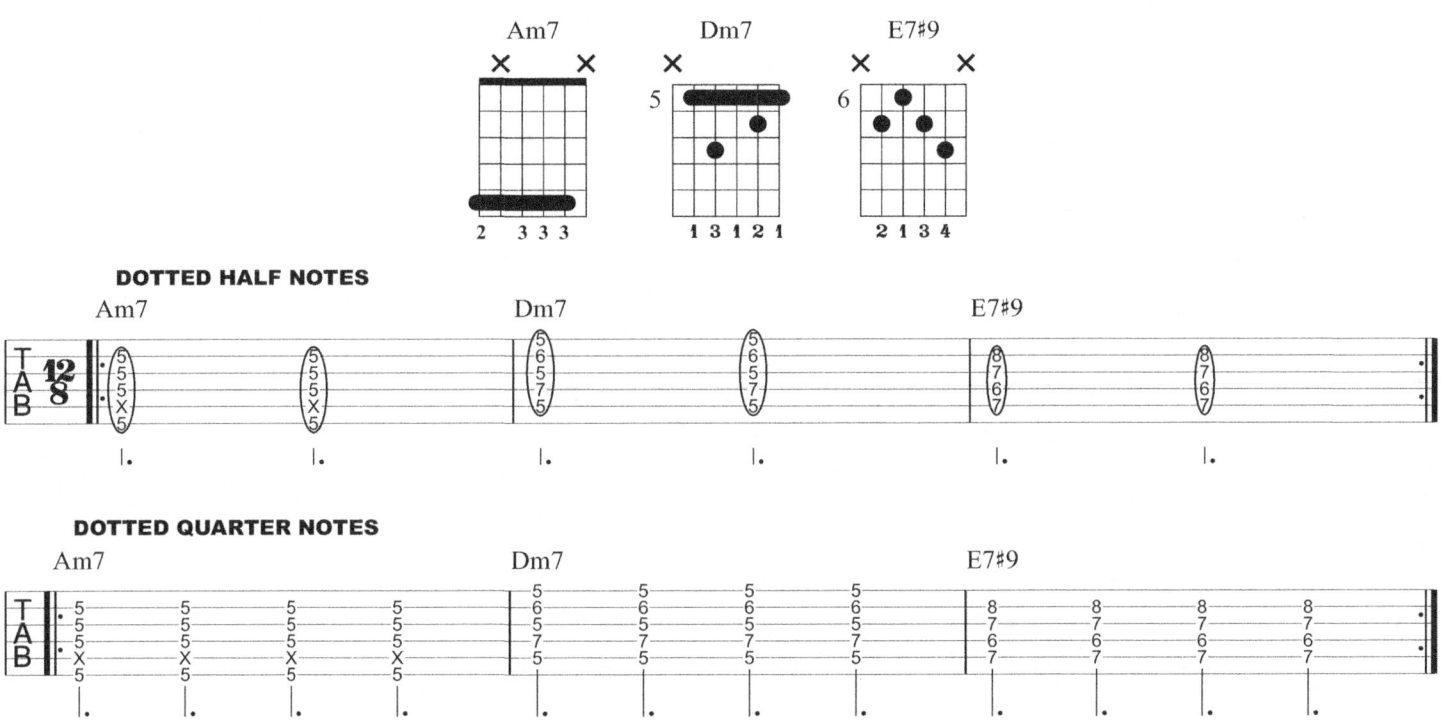

RHYTHM & HARMONY (1:15–1:00)

This rhythm figure is in the style of a blues ballad. What really stands out here is the quick Dm7–E7#9 change that occurs in measure 2, as the V chord typically doesn't make an appearance until bar 9 of a 12-bar blues, and the V chord is often minor in quality in a minor blues. The Dm7–E7#9 change is tricky, so be sure to give it proper attention.

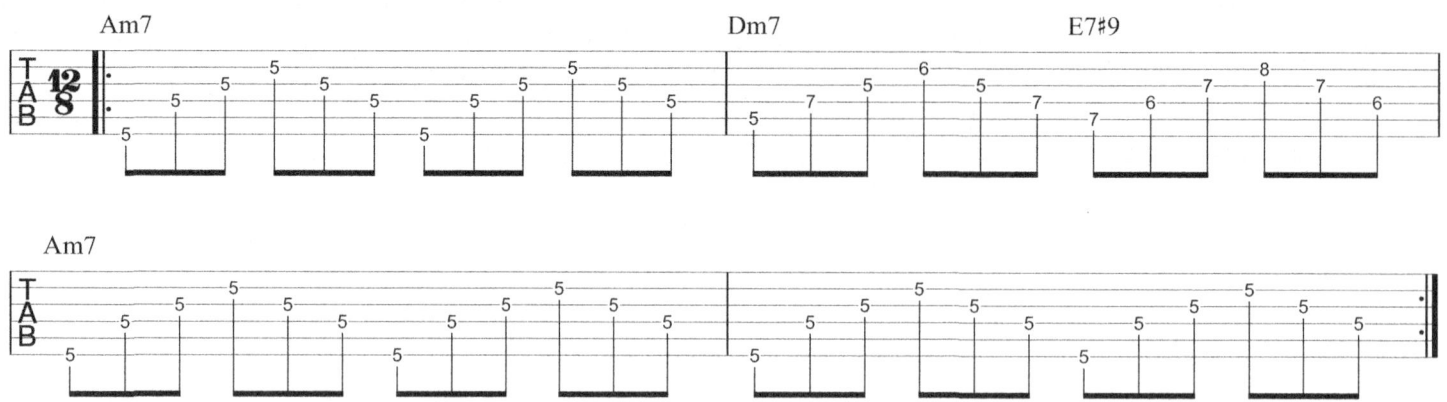

SCALE (1:00–0:45)

When a major or dominant seventh chord is substituted in place of a traditional minor (or minor seventh) v chord, we have to make special accommodations when soloing over it. The reason is pretty simple: the new chord—in our case, E7#9—has a major 3rd, G#, a note that's not found in our A minor pentatonic, A blues, or A natural minor scales (or E minor pentatonic, E blues, or E natural minor scales, for that matter), and therefore we cannot fully outline the E7#9 (V chord) harmony. The solution? We simply apply the A harmonic minor scale (A–B–C–D–E–F–G#), which will work over all three chords: Am7, Dm7, and E7#9 (theoretically, when A harmonic minor is played over E7#9, we are playing the fifth mode of the scale, E Phrygian dominant: E–F–G#–A–B–C–D).

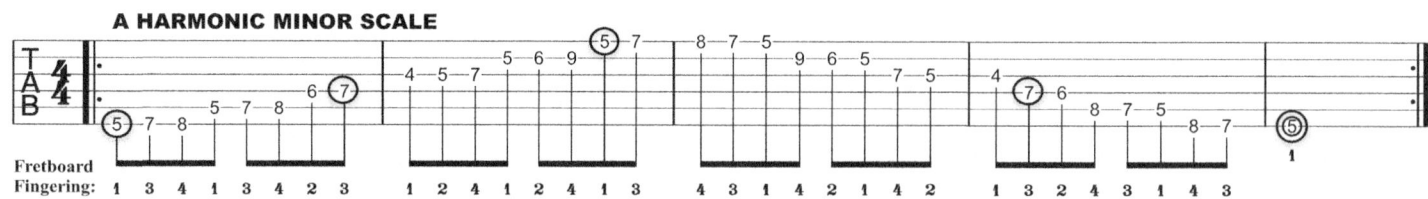

TECHNIQUE (0:45–0:30)

Palm muting is most typically associated with rhythm guitar playing, but the technique is quite effective in lead playing, too, especially when we want to emphasis particular notes. Below is a pair of exercises that use palm muting to accentuate certain notes of the A harmonic minor scale. To execute the palm mutes, simply rest the palm of your pick hand on the strings (near the bridge) while you pluck the notes with your pick, removing the palm for the quarter-step bends.

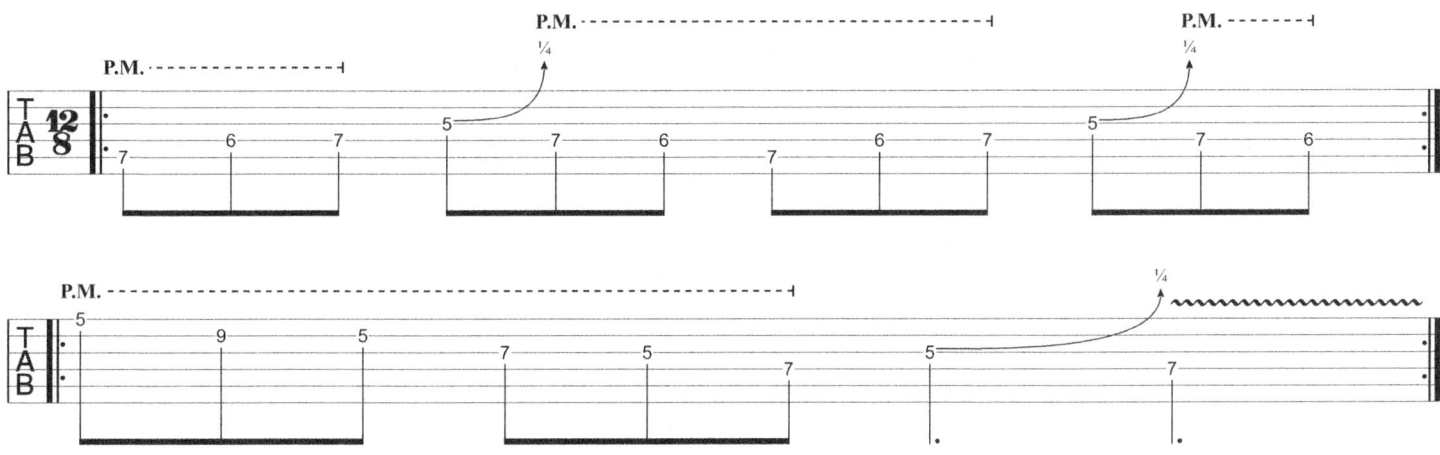

LEAD LICK (0:30–0:15)

Played over the Am7–Dm7–E7#9–Am7 progression from our arpeggiated blues-ballad rhythm figure, the four-bar lick below is rooted entirely in the A harmonic minor scale and features everything from quarter-step bends and vibrato to hammer-ons, pull-offs, and slides. Although some of the phrases have a distinct minor-pentatonic feel, the overall sound is wholly harmonic minor. One element of particular importance is found in bar 2, where the E7#9 is greeted with the defining pitch of A harmonic minor, G#, which also happens to be the major 3rd of the chord. It's a perfect example of a chord-scale relationship.

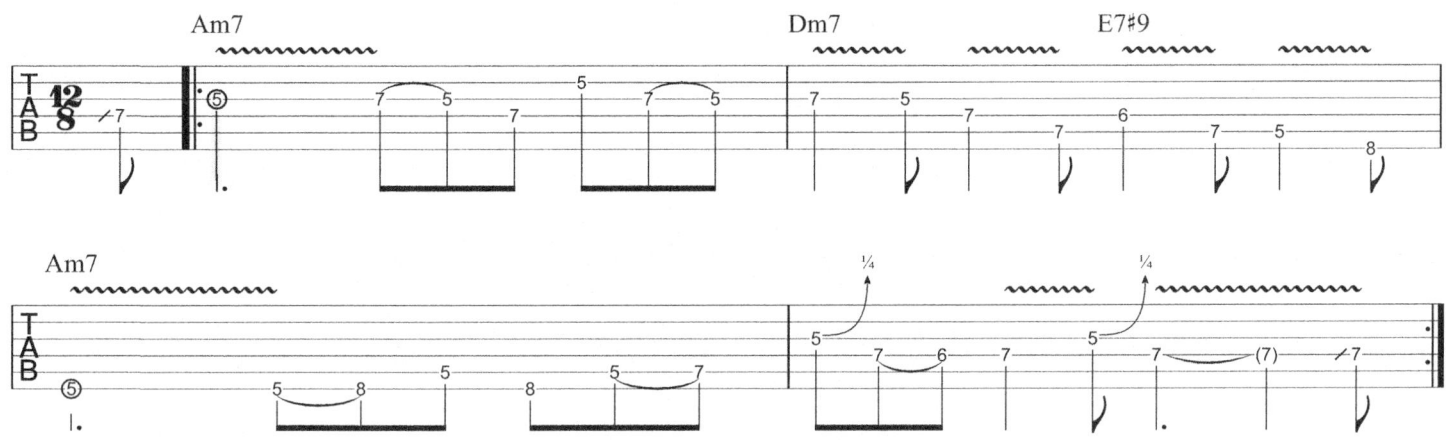

TURNAROUND (0:15–0:00)

Today's turnaround features our trusty i–iv–i–V (a minor-key version of the major I–IV–I–V) progression played entirely with arpeggios to match the blues-ballad rhythm that we learned in the Rhythm & Harmony section. Be sure to let all of the notes of the chords ring out fully.

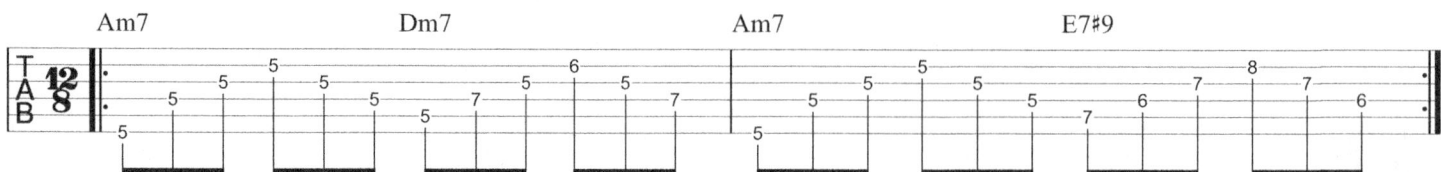

DAY 14

WEEK 2 REVIEW: PUTTING IT ALL TOGETHER (1:30–0:00)

We made it! After two weeks of hard work, we're ready to put in our final 90-minute practice session. Below is a full 12-bar solo like the one we played on Day 7. Here, we're playing over the arpeggiated blues-ballad rhythm that we learned yesterday, and the entire solo is performed with just two scales, A minor pentatonic and A harmonic minor, with the latter doing most of the heavy lifting.

After a pair of minor-pentatonic whole-step bends/releases in the pickup measure, the solo commences with a full measure of the root note, A, which is voiced here at fret 5 of string 1. Things pick up in bar 2, where the solo quickly descends the A harmonic minor/E Phrygian dominant scale. The rest of the solo follows a similar pattern, with moments of calm broken up by strings of unyielding eighth notes. Take note because this type of tension and release is a great way to keep your listeners' attention. When you get tired of practicing the solo, move on to the rhythm part, but spend a good chunk of time learning both.

Once you're finished with the book, be sure to come back to it from time to time. There's a ton of good information to digest and fun examples to play, and you'll most likely need more than 14 days of 90-minute practice sessions to comprehend it fully. Good luck!

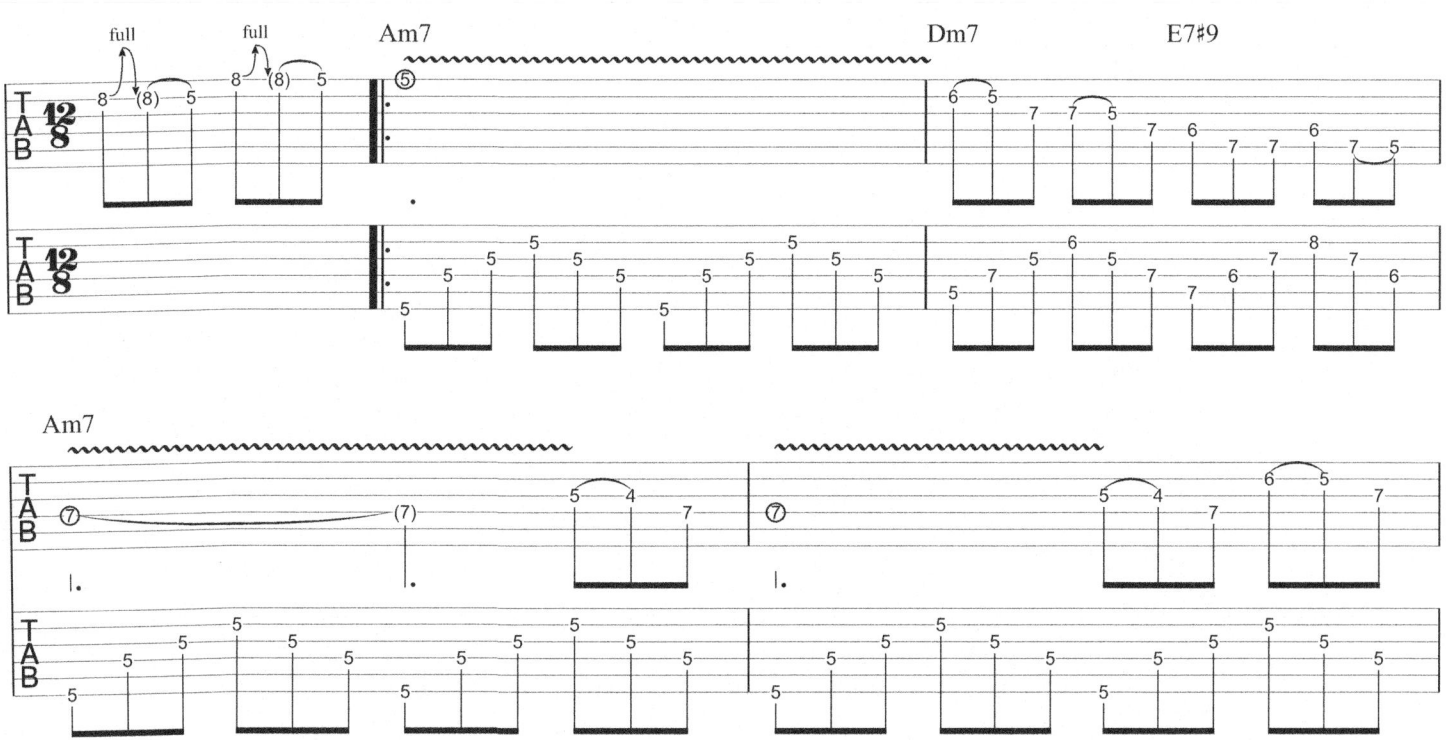

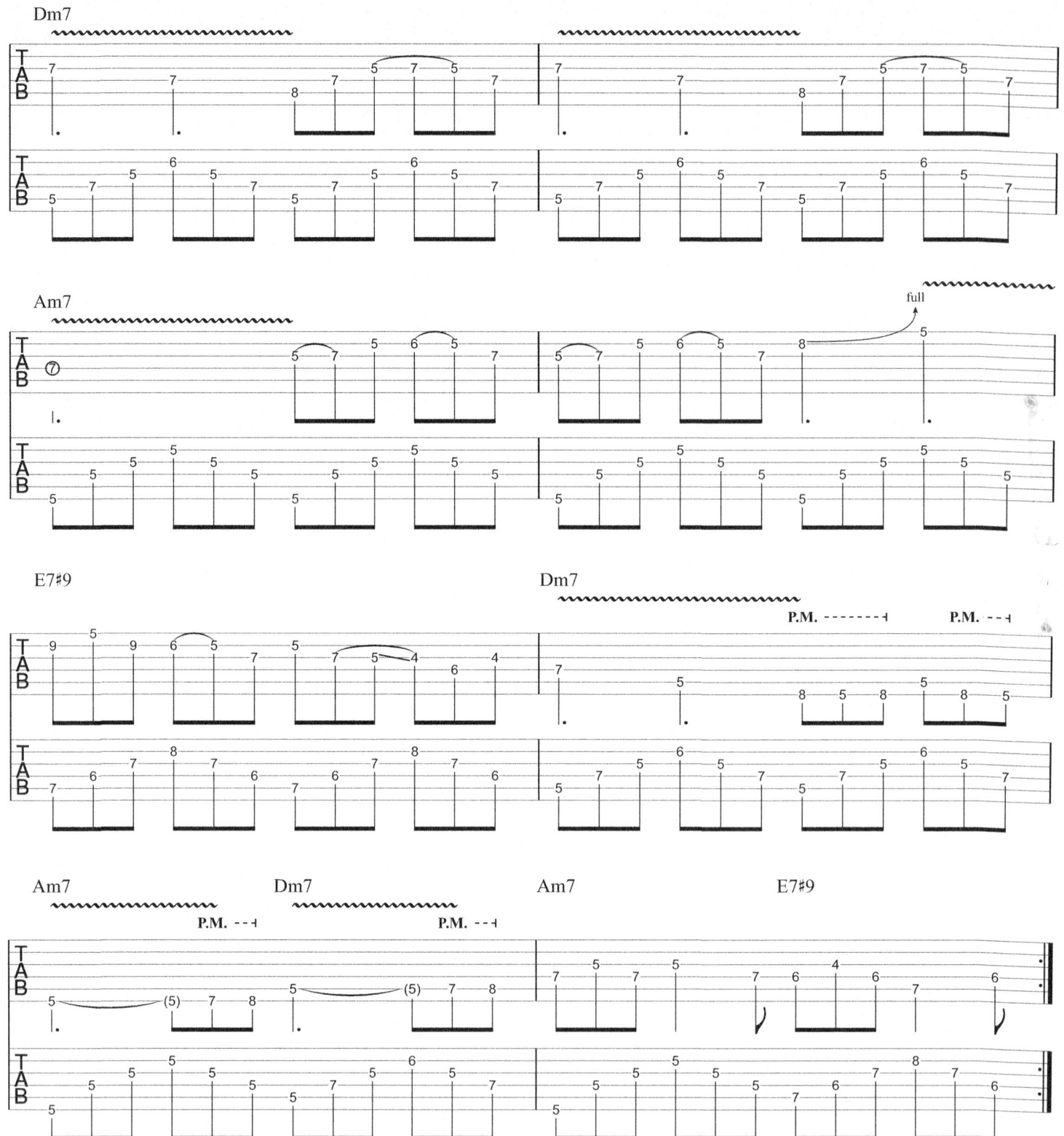

Printed in Great Britain
by Amazon